מגילת רות

FAITH
AND
FORTITUDE

MEGILLAT RUTH
AND
THE TORAH READING
FOR SHAVUOT

With Commentary from the Writings of
RABBI ELIEZER BERKOVITS

Compiled and Edited by
REUVEN MOHL

URIM PUBLICATIONS
Jerusalem • New York

Faith and Fortitude: Megillat Ruth and the Torah Reading for Shavuot
With Commentary from the Writings of Rabbi Eliezer Berkovits
Compiled and Edited by Reuven Mohl

Typeset by Juliet Tresgallo

Printed in the USA
First Edition
ISBN 978-1-60280-523-1

Urim Publications
P.O. Box 52287
Jerusalem 9152102 Israel
www.UrimPublications.com

KTAV Publishing House
527 Empire Boulevard
Brooklyn, NY 11225
www.ktav.com

Cataloging-in-Publication data is available from the Library of Congress.

Contents

*T*his Sefer is dedicated
לזכר נשמות

My husband

IRWIN PEYSER Z"L
הרב ישראל חיים בן דוד ופריידע רייזל ז"ל

My brother-in-law

PAUL PEYSER Z"L
פינחס בן דוד ופריידע רייזל ז"ל

My parents-in-law

DAVID & ROSE PEYSER Z"L
דוד בן פנחס ומינדל רבקה ז"ל
פריידע רייזל בת יהושע ושרה רבקה ז"ל

May their memory and commitment to the Torah values of
tzedakah and *chesed*, emphasized in Megillat Ruth, continue to inspire
our family for years to come.

BEATRICE PEYSER

Introduction

R ABBI ELIEZER BERKOVITS (1908–1992) was one of the major Jewish thinkers of the twentieth century. He was a renowned philosopher, theologian, and talmudic scholar. He studied under Rabbi Yechiel Yaakov Weinberg at the Hildesheimer Rabbinical Seminary in Berlin, and he received his Ph.D. in philosophy from the University of Berlin. He served in the rabbinate in Berlin (1934–1939), Leeds, England (1940–1946), Sydney, Australia (1946– 1950), and Boston (1950–1958). In 1958 he became chair of the philosophy department at the Hebrew Theological College in Skokie, and in 1976 he made *aliyah* to live the remainder of his life in Israel. In addition to his numerous philosophical writings and articles, he was the author of nineteen books including *Faith After the Holocaust*; *God, Man and History*; and *Not in Heaven: The Nature and Function of Halakha*. He also wrote two works on halacha that were published in Hebrew: *Conditionality in Marriage and Divorce* and *Halakha: Its Authority and Function*.

Rabbi Berkovits was a pioneer in examining many present-day crucial ideas within a halachic framework. He did not fear to express what he believed to be correct and ethical. His *T'nai Bi'N'suin u'V'Get* (*Conditionality in Marriage and Divorce*) attempted to solve the *aguna* crisis and his *Jewish Women in Time and Torah* described women's new place in our halachic community.

This book is the third in a series where I organize excerpts of Rabbi Berkovits' writings. The first was *Faith and Freedom*, a commentary to the Passover Haggadah that provides a popular entrée to Rabbi Berkovits' thoughts and concerns. The second volume, *Faith Fulfilled*, arranged a new collection of excerpts as a commentary to Megillat Esther and the Maariv prayer service. This volume, *Faith and Fortitude*, continues the project with different excerpts forming a novel commentary to Megillat Ruth and also the Torah reading for Shavuot. Through

this commentary, I hope the reader will gain a greater appreciation of Rabbi Berkovits' contributions and also enjoy reading a newly formed interpretation. A bibliography of the works from which the excerpts are drawn is to be found at the end of this volume.

There are few direct references to the book of Ruth throughout Rabbi Berkovits' writings. This commentary was formed by merging thematic connections between the text of Megillat Ruth and Rabbi Berkovits' writings, by attaching his thoughts to the texts, endeavoring to explain them through his words.

One of the rare occurrences where Rabbi Berkovits does directly quote and elaborate is from Ruth (2:4): "And behold, Boaz came from Bethlehem and said to the harvesters: God be with you."

> "It is time to act for God" (Tehillim 119:126) applies not only in matters directly connected with divine service, like the preservation of the Temple of Jerusalem. At times, it is permitted to suspend a biblical law even by an action whose purpose is altogether social. We read in a mishna: "It was established [by the sages] that one greet one's fellow man with the name of God. For thus we read in the Bible: 'And behold, Boaz came from Bethlehem and said to the harvesters: God be with you.'" This practice, reintroduced in mishnaic times, was not at all self-evident. According to the Torah, one must not take the name of God in vain. To justify this form of greeting, the mishna quotes the verse, "It is time to act for God," which one of its teachers, R. Natan, interprets: "Dissolve the law in order to act for God" (Brachot 54a). In this instance, the explanation of Rashi is most revealing. He writes: "At times one abolishes the words of the Torah in order to act for God. So this one, too, whose concern is with the well-being of his fellow man, is doing the will of God. For it is written, 'Seek peace and pursue it.' It is permissible to dissolve the Torah and do what appears to be forbidden." To some extent this is an exceptional case of "it is time to act for God." There is no real suspension of any law here. Because of a divine commandment, "Seek peace and pursue it," (Tehillim 34:15) one is actually urged to greet his neighbor with the Divine Name. Far from taking this name in vain, one actually does the will of God.
>
> *Not in Heaven*, pages 100–101

This excerpt contains many crucial and key points of Rabbi Berkovits'

philosophical thought. He explains that there really are no contesting and opposing obligations in this case. By greeting one's neighbor in the name of God, one is not defaming a Torah prohibition by saying God's name in vain, but actually obeying God's command of "Seek peace and pursue it." The directive of "it is time to act for God" expounded as dissolving a Torah law for social and other important considerations is a crucial tool used in the halachic process of Rabbi Berkovits. A Torah law is not being broken but instead upheld to its fullest.

There are many cases where Rabbi Berkovits elaborates and wishes that the Torah be utilized for the betterment and rectification for individuals and society. The Torah would be strengthened, not impaired or weakened, by highlighting a Torah principle that brings unity and peace. When discussing a difficult resolution to a case of *halitza*, he declares, "By God, this was not what the Torah meant! This was not halacha; certainly not 'ways of pleasantness and paths of peace!'" (*Not in Heaven*, page 160).

Writing on conversion, he insists, "The problem is that in this case the prescribed laws on conversion are in conflict with another important principle of Judaism, that of preserving the unity of Israel, the idea of *knesset Yisrael* through the obligation of *ahavat Yisrael*, the love for the people of Israel. Only when we understand this, have we raised the halachic question" (*Judaism*, page 469).

Rabbi Berkovits applies the unity principle when discussing women and *tefillah*. "Nothing could be more wrong than to assert that by holding their own services women separate themselves from the community. On the contrary, their own services in common bring them nearer to the experience of Jewish unity as intended by the Torah" (*Jewish Women in Time and Torah*, page 87).

It is interesting to note that Rabbi Yechiel Yaakov Weinberg employs "it is time to act for God" to permit women to sing *zemirot* at the Shabbat table. He also uses this injunction to allow mixed youth groups and to permit boys and girls to learn Torah together (*Sridei Eish* 2:8). Rabbi Berkovits was certainly influenced by his teacher.

Rabbi Berkovits wrote a lengthy article in 1986 entitled "Unity of Judaism" dealing with the increased polarization among Jewish religious groups. He advises that we need to change our way of thinking about the halachic process. By recognizing the importance of the unity of Israel as a Torah directive, we are following God's command and in no way relegating it.

Rabbi Berkovits clearly stresses the importance of unity:

One of the most serious problems of our day is the widespread ideological fragmentation within the Jewish people. The religious ideologies are numerous. Yet Judaism in its very essence is not sectarian but the way of life of a people. Indeed, it can be fully realized only by a people. To work for Jewish unity in the spirit of *ahavat Yisrael*, love for every Jew, in the interest of *klal Yisrael*, the reality of the totality of the Jewish people, is an urgent demand of Torah realization. Regrettably, rather than contributing to the striving for Jewish unity, halakha as understood today only deepens and fortifies the fragmentation.

It is our conviction that halakha must be stretched to its limits in order to further Jewish unity and mutual understanding. In the Orthodox camp, certain psychological impediments have to be overcome.

Not in Heaven, pages 160–161

Another important aspect of Rabbi Berkovits' philosophy that can be found in the above excerpt is God's presence in history, which is exemplified when Boaz greets his harvesters, "God be with You." In the second volume, *Faith Fulfilled*, I included my essay "Tsimtsum in the Writings of Rabbi Eliezer Berkovits," in which I explained Rabbi Berkovits' thoughts on Divine Self-limitation.

Over the years, I have come to understand that Rabbi Berkovits' idea of Divine Self-limitation is crucial and contingent on the idea of Divine Presence. Only because of His Self-limitation, is God able to be present.

One may pray only because one is able to believe that even after the act of creation, God has remained with the world, that indeed He renews daily the works of creation. One is able to believe this only within the context of revelational religion. We know of His presence, because He has made His presence known; we know that He is near, because He has indeed been near. We may turn to Him in prayer, because He has turned to man in revelation.

Prayer, page 73

Rabbi Berkovits' son, Rabbi Dov, shared his thoughts with me in response to a lecture I presented on the topic of *tsimstum*, at a conference dedicated in 2022 on the 30th anniversary of his father's yahrzeit.

For a long time there has been a very fundamental missing link in my understanding of the "prophetic encounter" which becomes the model for the Jewish experience of "history" and the shared human-divine responsibility for it.

What I now understand in a very few words is this:

1. Like Rambam, Hashem is infinite beyond human conception, "*ein sof*" etc. – that requires the concept of "separateness" between God and man.

2. Yet that belief and understanding does not allow for concern, involvement, and real prayer.

3. That's where there is the deep connection to Yehuda Halevi and the prophetic reality which is one of relationship, even fellowship – but that could lead as it does to what my father *z"l* criticized in the "pathos" of Heschel – and Christianity.

4. In order to understand how both are possible at the same time, my father *z"l* used kabbalistic ideas about *tsimtsum* from the Ari, (Rabbi Isaac Luria), and *chazal's* understanding of the name "*shadai*" to describe "self-abnegation" etc. and at the same time he distanced himself from the panentheism that the Kabbalah leads to because that does not allow for the possibility of real separateness which is critical for the possibility of relationship, concern, involvement and human freedom and responsibility.

In my understanding this construct is a real *chidush* in the history of Jewish philosophy and theology without which it is not possible to explain clearly what my father *z"l* referred to as the "religion of the *Tanach*."

It is important to reexamine Rabbi Berkovits' writings to gain insight into how to improve the world around us by implementing the unifying principles of the Torah as the catalyst for this advancement. Our conduct and performance will be transformed. Realizing God's presence and direct guidance will further enhance our accomplishments and achievements by urging us to act more fastidiously with constructive and effective results. By greeting others in God's name, by acting ethically in God's name, and by appreciating that God is near, we declare God's manifestation and thereby obey God's command, "It is time to act for God."

Rabbi Berkovits poignantly pleads with us:

As in the past, because it was a time to act for God, shackles had

to be placed on the Oral Torah in violation of God's command, so now the hour has come when the need to act for God places upon us the responsibility to free the Oral Torah from its shackles in obedience to God's original command. There are risks involved in such an undertaking. Because of it we need, not less, but more *yi'rat shammayim* (fear of God). But, possibly, most of all, we need to join much more *ahavat Yisrael* to our *ahavat ha-Torah*, by far more love of all Israel to illuminate our love of Torah. And pray to God for His guidance.

Judaism, page 478

Let us heed his advice and live up to his words!

I am truly thankful to Professor Avraham Berkovits and Rabbi Dov Berkovits, sons of Rabbi Eliezer Berkovits *z"l*, for their ongoing encouragement and approval.

Thank you to Beatrice Peyser for generously sponsoring this volume in memory of her husband, Irwin Peyser *z"l*, her brother-in-law, Paul Peyser *z"l*, and her parents-in-law, David and Rose Peyser *z"l*. May their memory be a blessing.

Thank you to Tzvi Mauer of Urim Publications for his friendly assistance and to Pearl Friedman for her excellent proofreading.

I owe a special thank you to Dr. Joel Wolowelsky for his continued confidence and much appreciated advice. I wish him much happiness on his *Aliya*.

Thank you to Dr. Ari Kinsberg, for our close friendship, sharing his vast scholarship, and for reviewing the final proofs.

Thank you to my sister and brother-in-law, Rachel and Dr. Stuart Abrahams, for our close relationship.

Finally, I express a tremendous amount of thanks, love, and gratitude to:

My parents, Shelly and Rabbi Oscar Mohl, my source of advice, wisdom, and love. I wish them only health and *nachat* from their family.

My children, Dahlia, Nate, and Sammy, my pride and inspiration. I wish Dahlia and Nate much success and *mazal* in Israel.

My wife, Jennie, my best friend, confidant, and partner. I wish her the best of everything.

Hodu LaHashem!

Reuven Mohl
Teaneck, New Jersey
January 2024/Shevat 5784

מגילת רות

FAITH
AND
FORTITUDE

MEGILLAT RUTH
AND
THE TORAH READING
FOR SHAVUOT

מְגִילַת רוּת

פרק א

וַיְהִי בִּימֵי שְׁפֹט הַשֹּׁפְטִים וַיְהִי רָעָב בָּאָרֶץ וַיֵּלֶךְ אִישׁ מִבֵּית לֶחֶם יְהוּדָה

---

judges judged   שְׁפֹט הַשֹּׁפְטִים

We are now in a position to understand a rather unusual title that the leaders of the Jewish people had at a certain time in history. After Joshua, and up to the election of Saul to kingship, the leaders of Israel were called judges. But why judges? They were of course judges, too, but that was not their chief function. They were the heads of the people, fulfilling the function that later on was that of the kings. It is rather strange that they should have been called judges. However, it is strange only if for us the meaning of the word is its meaning in the English language. The title, however, is quite proper if we attempt to think in biblical terms. What does the Bible say about the judges?

And the Lord raised up *judges*, who *saved* them out of the hand of those that spoiled them. ... And when the Lord raised them up *judges*, then the Lord was with the judge, and *saved* them out of the hand of their enemies all the days of the judge (Judges 2:16,18).

This makes, of course, very poor sense in English. Since when is it the task of judges to save their people out of the hand of their enemies? This sounds altogether different in Hebrew, especially as one recalls that instead of, "who saved them out of the hand of those that spoiled them," one could almost say, who judged them out of their hands; or as one remembers that, as we saw, Isaiah uses *mishpat* (judgment) and *yeshu'ah* (salvation, deliverance) as parallels. Since to judge in Hebrew may well mean to save, the judge may well be the savior or the one through whom God sends deliverance to His people. How inseparable is the function of the judge from that of the savior comes to magnifi-

16

MEGILLAT RUTH

In the days when the **judges judged**, **there was a famine in the land**; and a man of Bethlehem in Judah, with his wife and two sons,

---

cent expression in the words of Isaiah: For the Lord is our Judge, The Lord is our Lawgiver, The Lord is our King; He will save us (33:22).

Man and God, pages 234–235

There was a famine in the land   וַיְהִי רָעָב בָּאָרֶץ

There is a famine in the land, not a famine of bread nor a thirst for water, but of hearing the words of God. Not that "hunger for bread and thirst for water" do not exist, but perhaps external, economic, and political insecurity is needed to make man fully aware of his human condition, of his spiritual starvation. The signs of this "famine" may be observed by all who care to look for them. In my own experience, I notice it by the subjects on which Jews of all "denominations" wish to hear lectures and attend classes. They are: Jewish ethics as applied to the manifold concerns of contemporary man, and most surprisingly – Talmud, Talmud, Talmud, and, of course, faith after the holocaust, with the emphasis on faith, faith, faith.

These are the questions of destiny directed to us in this hour:

Do we have a full understanding of the nature of this hunger? Do we have the capacity to satisfy it? Can we provide the new foundations, the new anchor? Are we able to reconstruct a world of values, of faith and hope for our people? Can we do it from the sources of Judaism?

The task is twofold: a) intellectual-spiritual; b) psychological-emotional. Let us consider the first part first. Whether they like it or not, once Jews left the ghettos, they have been living in continuous

לָגוּר֙ בִּשְׂדֵ֣י מוֹאָ֔ב ה֥וּא וְאִשְׁתּ֖וֹ וּשְׁנֵ֥י בָנָֽיו: ²וְשֵׁ֣ם הָאִ֣ישׁ אֱלִימֶ֡לֶךְ וְשֵׁם֩ אִשְׁתּ֨וֹ נָעֳמִ֜י וְשֵׁ֣ם שְׁנֵֽי־בָנָ֣יו ׀ מַחְל֤וֹן וְכִלְיוֹן֙ אֶפְרָתִ֔ים מִבֵּ֥ית לֶ֖חֶם יְהוּדָ֑ה וַיָּבֹ֥אוּ שְׂדֵי־מוֹאָ֖ב וַיִּֽהְיוּ־שָֽׁם: ³וַיָּ֥מָת אֱלִימֶ֖לֶךְ אִ֣ישׁ נָעֳמִ֑י וַתִּשָּׁאֵ֥ר הִ֖יא וּשְׁנֵ֥י בָנֶֽיהָ: ⁴וַיִּשְׂא֣וּ לָהֶ֗ם נָשִׁים֙ מֹֽאֲבִיּ֔וֹת שֵׁ֤ם הָֽאַחַת֙ עָרְפָּ֔ה וְשֵׁ֥ם הַשֵּׁנִ֖ית ר֑וּת וַיֵּ֥שְׁבוּ שָׁ֖ם

---

confrontation with another culture and civilization. If now, in this hour of the exhaustion of this culture, there is a search for standards and values, for new spiritual foundations, and if we are to respond to this search effectively, we must understand that culture and civilization critically; we must understand wherein it has failed and why. We must find the strength to cast the searching darkness of man's contemporary predicament, of his present-day spiritual confusion and despair, on the sources of Judaism, and make them light up, as once the *Urim ve Tumim* lit up in response to the searching questions of the High Priest. It requires consistent study and hard work to unlock the response of the Torah to the problems of our time. It demands a sympathetic and penetrating understanding of those problems, as well as the ability to bring the wisdom of the Torah to bear on those problems in such a manner that the searching mind may find intellectual and emotional peace. We dare not be just demanding in the name of the Torah; we have to be convincing with the truth of the Torah.

Crisis and Faith, pages 167–168

in the country of Moab   בִּשְׂדֵי מוֹאָב

Even Moses is not a sacrificial hero in Judaism. His death is not wrapped in the mantle of the tragic so that it should inspire and be revered by future generations. There is no death stance of Moses. He went up to the mountain of Nebo from where God showed him the land into which he was not to enter. He died there in the land of Moab as God had spoken. "And he buried him in the land of Moab... and no one knows his burial place to this day" (Deuteronomy 34:5–7). According to a midrashic commentary, (see Rashi) Moses died by a kiss of God, by which the rabbis meant to say that death was not only the end of Moses' life, but its conclusion. The legacy he left behind is his life, not his death. Even the *akedah*, the near-sacrifice of Isaac by Abraham, which has a place in Judaism similar to the sacrifice of Jesus in Christianity,

went to reside **in the country of Moab**. [2] The man's name was
Elimelech, his wife's name was Naomi, and his two sons were named
Mahlon and Chilion – Ephrathites of Bethlehem in Judah. **They
came to the country of Moab and remained there**. [3] Elimelech,

---

ends with a celebration of life. Abraham is being tested, but Isaac is to
live, an indication that while to obey God's command should be the
ultimate concern of the Jew, the purpose is not death but life.

That life itself is a fundamental value, that it should be defended even
at the risk of losing it, need not be argued. That life is holy and therefore
must not be destroyed, but rather protected, is essential Jewish teaching. However, *Kiddush haChayim* is not just the acknowledgment of the
holiness of life, but the deed of its sanctification. Life as such is given to
man; its sanctification is the task of man.

With God in Hell, pages 103–104

וַיָּבֹאוּ שְׂדֵי־מוֹאָב וַיִּהְיוּ־שָׁם

They came to the country of Moab and remained there

The shifting of the "Jewish Geography" brings in its wake the disorgani-
zation of the spiritual structure of Judaism. It is a mistake to think that
Judaism can be transported – as it were – from one country to another.
Judaism is not a book or a library which you may carry with you from
one place to another. Judaism is not a mere theoretical system, a com-
pilation of ideals and beliefs. Judaism is life lived by Jews, it is a system
of purposes and intentions, carried into realization by living Jewries.
The great Russian Jewry, with its own history, its own traditions, its
Russo-Jewish propensities, and idiosyncrasies, represented Judaism. In
its dissolution, Judaism also dissolved. Polish and German Jewry, in all
their activities, communal organizations, religious-cultural institutions,
and in their particular style of thinking and living, represented various
historic shapes of living Judaism. In its disintegration, Judaism went
under, and in its disappearance, Judaism vanished.

One cannot replant the Judaism of one country in the soil of another.
Every Jewry is unique. The shape that Judaism takes in the various Jewries is always "locally" determined. The Jewish emigrant always carries
with him only the ruins of his former spiritual existence, the ruins of
Judaism as lived in his own native Jewry, just as he carries in his little

כַּאֲשֶׁר שָׁנִים: ⁵וַיָּמֻתוּ גַם־שְׁנֵיהֶם מַחְלוֹן וְכִלְיוֹן וַתִּשָּׁאֵר הָאִשָּׁה מִשְּׁנֵי יְלָדֶיהָ
וּמֵאִישָׁהּ: ⁶וַתָּקָם הִיא וְכַלֹּתֶיהָ וַתָּשָׁב מִשְּׂדֵי מוֹאָב כִּי שָׁמְעָה בִּשְׂדֵה מוֹאָב
כִּי־פָקַד יְהֹוָה אֶת־עַמּוֹ לָתֵת לָהֶם לָחֶם: ⁷וַתֵּצֵא מִן־הַמָּקוֹם אֲשֶׁר הָיְתָה־
שָׁמָּה וּשְׁתֵּי כַלֹּתֶיהָ עִמָּהּ וַתֵּלַכְנָה בַדֶּרֶךְ לָשׁוּב אֶל־אֶרֶץ יְהוּדָה: ⁸וַתֹּאמֶר
נָעֳמִי לִשְׁתֵּי כַלֹּתֶיהָ לֵכְנָה שֹּׁבְנָה אִשָּׁה לְבֵית אִמָּהּ (יעשה) יַעַשׂ יְהֹוָה
עִמָּכֶם חֶסֶד כַּאֲשֶׁר עֲשִׂיתֶם עִם־הַמֵּתִים וְעִמָּדִי: ⁹יִתֵּן יְהֹוָה לָכֶם וּמְצֶאןָ

---

bundle the miserable remnants of his former material existence.

As soon as the Polish or Lithuanian Jew leaves his country, he ceased to be the Polish or Lithuanian Jew. He became the former Polish or Lithuanian Jew. He became the shadow of the Polish or Lithuanian Jew, the shadow of a historic Jewish type.

This is the real tragedy of the Jews who were forced out of the countries of their historic sojournings into the Wilderness of the Nations.

Between Yesterday and Tomorrow, pages 118–119

the Lord had taken note of His people   כִּי־פָקַד יְהֹוָה אֶת־עַמּוֹ

God's unconvincing presence in history is testified through the survival of Israel. All God's miracles occur outside of history. When God acts with manifest power, history is at a standstill. The only exception to the rule is the historic reality of Israel. That "faith history" has not been erased from the face of the earth by "power history," notwithstanding the incalculable material superiority of the forces arrayed against it throughout the ages, is the ultimate miracle. Since, however, it has been accomplished without manifest divine intervention, the miracle of the viability of faith remains within history. It is for this reason that Isaiah could say of Israel on behalf of God: "Therefore you are My witnesses, saith the Eternal, and I am God" (Isaiah 43:12). The rabbis rightly add the comment: If you are my witnesses, I am God; if you do not witness, I am – as it were – no God. There is no other witness that God is present in history other than the history of the Jewish people. God's own destiny in history is joined to the history of Israel. Great empires do not testify to the Divine Presence in history. Whatever they are and accomplish is fully explicable in terms of their material resources. They have their self-explanatory place in "power history." Half a billion

Naomi's husband, died; and she was left with her two sons. ⁴ They married Moabite women, one named Orpah and the other Ruth, and they lived there about ten years. ⁵ Then those two – Mahlon and Chilion – also died; so the woman was left without her two sons and without her husband. ⁶ She started out with her daughters-in-law to return from the country of Moab; for in the country of Moab she had heard that **the Lord had taken note of His people** and given them food. ⁷ Accompanied by her two daughters-in-law, she left the place where she had been living; and they set out on the road back to the land of Judah. ⁸ But Naomi said to her two daughters-in-law, "Turn back, each of you to her mother's house. **May the Lord deal kindly with you**, as you have dealt with the dead and with me!

Christians all over the world prove nothing about God's presence in history. They are too many, too influential, too pervasive. They are a materialistic, this-worldly, power in the context of "power history." The same is true of any of the other great world religions. They have too many followers, too much territorial control, and too many resources of influence and power to prove anything. God is a mere adjunct to their position in history. Their religious affirmatives are incidental to their position in history. They all function in "power history." Only a small people whose very existence is forever assailed by the forces of "power history" and yet survive and have an impact on world history, completely out of proportion to its numbers and its material power, proves the validity of another dimension of reality and testifies to God's "powerless" guidance in the affairs of men. God's own destiny in history is linked to the history of Israel. Only by means of Israel may his, of necessity, unconvincing presence in history be surmised.

Faith After the Holocaust, pages 117–118

May the Lord deal kindly with you　　　יַעַשׂ יְהוָה עִמָּכֶם חֶסֶד

This refers to the personal God one may know only from His revelations, from His manifestations in the life of individuals or people. History is the foundation of all praying. In discussing the most intimately personal aspect of prayer, the outpouring of the heart, we had to connect with the historic experience of the community in order to resolve the dilemma of the confrontation. We saw how out of the depth of his

מְנוּחָה אִשָּׁה בֵּית אִישָׁהּ וַתִּשַּׁק לָהֶן וַתִּשֶּׂאנָה קוֹלָן וַתִּבְכֶּינָה: יֵוַתֹּאמַרְנָה־
לָהּ כִּי־אִתָּךְ נָשׁוּב לְעַמֵּךְ: יֵאוַתֹּאמֶר נָעֳמִי שֹׁבְנָה בְנֹתַי לָמָּה תֵלַכְנָה עִמִּי
הַעוֹד־לִי בָנִים בְּמֵעַי וְהָיוּ לָכֶם לַאֲנָשִׁים: יֵבשֹׁבְנָה בְנֹתַי לֵכְןָ כִּי זָקַנְתִּי

---

being personally forsaken by God, the individual Jew may yet call God
as if he confronted the Presence, because he is sustained all the time, in
the teeth of his personal history, by the historic experience of Israel and
of the ever-present God. The Jew may pray significantly on the spur
of the moment because he is sustained by the Jewish awareness of the
Divine Presence through time. It is the same collective experience of
all Israel that makes it possible for the Jew to formulate conceptually
those universal principles which are incorporated in obligatory prayer.
We cannot derive from any theology or philosophy, nor can we know
from a merely individual history, that God is forever present for man,
and that man is ever dependent and sustained by Him. Jews know this
on the strength of Israel's connection with God. Only on the basis of
the historical history of the Jewish people can a Jew meaningfully affirm that God is Provider, Healer, Redeemer, and Shield. Only because
of that history does a Jew know that His mercies and lovingkindness
are without an end, only on its strength can a Jew praise Him. One
cannot take a stand on a theology and pray; one can only pray in the
historic context of one's life with God. The purely individual history is
necessary, it provides prayer with depth of emotion, but it is inadequate.
Obligatory prayer is required to meet the inadequacies of free praying.
This obligatory prayer is founded on the historic experience of the Jewish people.

Prayer, pages 52–53

we will return with you to your people   כִּי־אִתָּךְ נָשׁוּב לְעַמֵּךְ

How to convert to Judaism is not a halachic problem. It is all stated
clearly in the Shulchan Aruch. The problem is that in this case, the
prescribed laws on conversion conflict with another important principle of Judaism, that of preserving the unity of Israel, the idea of *knesset
Yisrael*, through the obligation of *ahavat Yisrael*, the love for the people
of Israel. Only when we understand this, have we raised the halachic
question. For, indeed, such is the classical halachic "problem": That the

[8] May the Lord grant that each of you find security in the house of a husband!" And she kissed them farewell. They broke into weeping [10] and said to her, "No, **we will return with you to your people**." [11] But Naomi replied, "Turn back, my daughters! Why should you go with me? Have I any more sons in my body who might be husbands for you? [12] Turn back, my daughters, for I am too old to be married.

---

strict adherence to one law conflicts with the strict adherence to another obligatory principle of Judaism. In the case at hand, any Orthodox Jew has the right to say that for him, the importance of the laws of conversion are so vital that for their sake he will push aside all the important obligations regarding the concept of unity of Israel and love of Israel. But where does he find the authoritative basis for his decision? In the Shulchan Aruch, in the section on conversion? Certainly not. There he will find all the rules on how to convert a non-Jew. What he will not find there is the answer to our problem of halacha, i.e., in view of the importance of the idea of the unity of Israel and all that it involves. For according to the Torah, what should be our attitude to a vast number of fellow Jews who do not observe the laws of conversion as we do? Where, then, will he find the answer to his question, in which book, in which code? In no book, in no code. He must make this decision by himself, in his own Jewish conscience. But how so? He will accept the authoritative validity of the law on conversion, and at the same time he will acknowledge the importance of the unity and love of Israel; he will then seek resolution of the conflict from within the comprehensive ethos of Judaism, from what Judaism is about in its totality, according to his understanding and commitment. Moreover, this is an understanding and commitment which has grown into a measure of maturity as the result of the dedicated study of the classical sources of Judaism and of adherence to a way of life inseparable from it. This is not a purely subjective decision but just because of the subjective element involved in it, it will be a truly halachic solution to a genuinely halachic problem.

Conversion 'According to Halachah' – What Is It? *Judaism*, page 469

מִהְיוֹת לְאִישׁ כִּי אָמַרְתִּי יֶשׁ־לִי תִקְוָה גַּם הָיִיתִי הַלַּיְלָה לְאִישׁ וְגַם
יָלַדְתִּי בָנִים: יֹהֲלָהֵן ׀ תְּשַׂבֵּרְנָה עַד אֲשֶׁר יִגְדָּלוּ הֲלָהֵן תֵּעָגֵנָה לְבִלְתִּי
הֱיוֹת לְאִישׁ אַל בְּנֹתַי כִּי־מַר־לִי מְאֹד מִכֶּם כִּי־יָצְאָה בִי יַד־יְהוָֹה:

---

hope   תִקְוָה

I believe that Judaism knows man fairly well; it also knows history and understands it, and because of this, Judaism declares: "Not by might, nor by power, but by my spirit."

This is, indeed, our comfort, this is our hope. Not the comfort of weakness, nor the hope of despair; but the comfort of fortitude and the hope of strength.

Hope comes of strength, it is justified, when there is faith behind it. And it is the entire faith of Judaism that is the foundation of our hope for the ultimate victory of the spirit. It is our faith in God that stands behind it. Faith in God involves faith in life, it means faith in the ultimate value of life, in a moral purpose, slowly but surely realizing itself in life. Faith tells us that this world has been created by Him not for the purpose of being destroyed by the devil. Faith in God declares that the world can never be delivered to the ravaging powers of darkness and destruction.

Our faith in God, our trust in reason, our confidence in life, our unshakable belief in a moral purpose of history, all this has been summed up in the courageous words: "Not by might, nor by power, but by my spirit, saith the Lord" (Zechariah 4:6). For us, who are Jews, this is the very essence of life. If these words do not hold true, life itself is nothing but a horrible nightmare. If the spirit will not conquer, life itself must perish. If justice is to succumb, mankind will be wiped out. If truth is not to be victorious, the whole of the Universe must disintegrate, fall to pieces, and vanish in the void.

Our faith in the ultimate victory of the spirit is unshakable. It is as strong as life is, and it will last as long as life will last on earth.

Between Yesterday and Tomorrow, pages 10–11

anchor yourselves to man   תֵּעָגֵנָה לְבִלְתִּי הֱיוֹת לְאִישׁ

In general, the rule was that only witnesses who were able to read and write were allowed to testify on any document. Yet, in the case of divorce

Even if I thought there was **hope** for me, even if I were married tonight and I also bore sons, ¹³ Should you wait for them to grow up? Should you on their account **anchor yourselves to a man**? Oh no, my daughters! My lot is far more bitter than yours, **for the hand of God has struck out against me**." ¹⁴ They raised their voices and

---

documents, Rabbi Simeon ben Gamliel ruled that "with witnesses who cannot read, one reads for them and they sign. And with witnesses who are unable to sign, one scratches the shape of the letters of their names on the paper, which they can fill in afterward with ink" (Gittin 19b).

It would seem that this latter law, where the witnesses just fill in ink in the places prepared for them, goes much further than the one where the text of the get is read to the witnesses who can, at least, sign with their own handwriting. These arrangements, which are in fact contrary to important laws of adequate testimony, were instituted, says Rabbi Elazar, so that the daughters of Israel would not become agunot. The reason was that the husband might want to leave urgently for another land or a distant place. If no other witnesses were immediately available, he might depart without divorcing his wife. She would then be an agunah, "anchored" to a man who in fact no longer lives with her as a husband.

Jewish Women in Time and Torah, page 111

for the hand of God has struck out against me   כִּי־יָצְאָה בִי יַד־יְהוָה

The problem that often occupies man's mind is, however, not that God is a judge who is too exacting, executing justice without mercy and charity, but rather that he seems to be so often indifferent toward the evil perpetrated by man and the suffering of the innocent. It is not the task of this study to discuss the age-old theological problem of theodicy. However, one classical version of theodicy has a direct bearing on our immediate subject. It is the version which is found in Job. The story is well-known. Job queries the justice of God. One ought to appreciate the seriousness of Job's inner struggle. His undeserved suffering is not his chief preoccupation, nor the self-righteous affirmation of his innocence. His concern is with the nature of God. How can God be unjust? It is the most serious problem that may perturb a believing soul. It is for this reason that he must reject all the arguments of his friends. The

יד וַתִּשֶּׂנָה קוֹלָן וַתִּבְכֶּינָה עוֹד וַתִּשַּׁק עָרְפָּה לַחֲמוֹתָהּ וְרוּת דָּבְקָה
בָּהּ: טו וַתֹּאמֶר הִנֵּה שָׁבָה יְבִמְתֵּךְ אֶל־עַמָּהּ וְאֶל־אֱלֹהֶיהָ שׁוּבִי אַחֲרֵי
יְבִמְתֵּךְ: טז וַתֹּאמֶר רוּת אַל־תִּפְגְּעִי־בִי לְעָזְבֵךְ לָשׁוּב מֵאַחֲרָיִךְ כִּי
אֶל־אֲשֶׁר תֵּלְכִי אֵלֵךְ וּבַאֲשֶׁר תָּלִינִי אָלִין עַמֵּךְ עַמִּי וֵאלֹהַיִךְ אֱלֹהָי:

---

issue is a fundamental issue of religious faith. It must not be blurred over with pious words. How can God be unjust?! And we who read the book and know from the introduction what was hidden from the eyes of Job, also know that what was done to Job was not justice. Demanding justice of God, Job is the great hero of faith who struggles for the honor of his God. He will not rest until he is given an answer, until he understands. For it cannot be, it must not be, that God should not act justly; and yet, he has experienced injustice at the hand of God.

Man and God, page 248

But Ruth clung to her   וְרוּת דָּבְקָה בָּהּ

Religion, in the understanding of Judaism, is based on acknowledging the reality of a personal God, a God who after creation did not leave this world, who continues to be involved in the destinies of His creatures, who is concerned about man, a God who cares, to whom we may turn in prayer and who responds to man's call; a God who stands in relationship to His world and who enters into covenants with man. But how does one know of such a God? Surely not through the power of reason, but through experience. A care, a concern has to be experienced or it does not exist. A covenant must be a form of actual relationship or it is a sham. The source of religion is in experience and not in reason. Is religion irrational then? One might as well ask if the gravitational pull between masses of matter is irrational. It does exist and it can be described in exact mathematical formulae, but it is certainly not rational. Facts do not have to validate themselves in the court of reason. This is even truer in the realm of interpersonal relationships. Friendship, love! Nothing could be more absurd than the idea that they have their origin in reason. Are they therefore irrational? They are neither rational nor irrational. There are ideas, concepts, and intellectual preoccupations that have to claim their validity through the categories of reason. And there are facts unto whom it is sufficient that they are, such as the laws of

broke into weeping again, and Orpah kissed her mother-in-law farewell. **But Ruth clung to her**. [15] So she said, "See, your sister-in-law has returned to her people and her gods. Go follow your sister-in-law." [16] But Ruth replied, "Do not urge me to leave you, to turn back and not follow you. **For wherever you go, I will go**; wherever you lodge, I will lodge; **your people shall be my people, and your God my God**.

---

nature. All they need is an exact description. Interpersonal relationships are living reality, existing by the strength of mutual acceptance in which two persons are covenanted to each other.

With God in Hell, pages 120–121

For wherever you go, I will go   כִּי אֶל־אֲשֶׁר תֵּלְכִי אֵלֵךְ

The essence of the Oral Torah is the halacha. As the root of the word (*haloch* walk, go) indicates, halacha teaches the way along which the Jew is required to walk in accordance with the Torah. Halacha is the application of the Torah to life. But since there is no such thing as life in general, since it is always a certain form of life at a specific time in history, in a specific situation, Torah application means application to a specific time in a specific situation. The result of this process is what I call halachic Judaism.

Not in Heaven, Introduction

עַמֵּךְ עַמִּי וֵאלֹהַיִךְ אֱלֹהָי
your people shall be my people, and your God my God

A nation's historical role is enacted on a level different from the realm of the individual religious confession. The deed, however, always takes place in the public realm. Faith is entertained in isolation. Indeed, the deeper the faith, the more private it is. The deed is impossible in isolation. It always affects others, it impinges on their lives, and it always refers beyond the boundaries of isolated individuality. Faith is the preoccupation of the soul. The deed is enacted by the entire person. Faith links the soul to God; the faith-informed deed links the whole person to the fellow man by way of God. Faith fills the soul; the deed, history. While by faith alone a soul may be saved, perhaps, the deed's *raison d'être* is to be effective in the world. For the sake of its effectiveness, the

יבַּאֲשֶׁר תָּמוּתִי אָמוּת וְשָׁם אֶקָּבֵר כֹּה יַעֲשֶׂה יְהוָה לִי וְכֹה יוֹסִיף כִּי
הַמָּוֶת יַפְרִיד בֵּינִי וּבֵינֵךְ:

---

deed will seek for its realization a group that is moved by a common faith and united by a common cause. The extent of the group depends on the area within which the deed is to be enacted. So it is with every idea that aspires to enter the world in the form of the human deed. The boundaries of the group will be determined by the area that the deed aims to occupy. But what if the fruition of the idea as the deed encompasses the whole of human existence? What if the faith seeks realization in economics, morals, politics, and in every manifestation of human life? In that case, the group ought to be all-comprehensive. Such a group should be mankind.

But mankind is not a group; it is not a historical entity. Mankind itself is an idea, an ideal. The comprehensive group to be created to suit the comprehensive deed as a historical reality is a people in sovereign control of the major areas of its life. The faith of Judaism requires such a comprehensive deed. Realization through and within the all-comprehensive collective, mankind, is the ideal; the instrument of its realization in history is the people. Since our concern is with the comprehensive deed of Judaism, the people is Israel. Of necessity, the covenant had to create the people with whom the covenant was concluded.

Faith After the Holocaust, pages 152–153

בַּאֲשֶׁר תָּמוּתִי אָמוּת וְשָׁם אֶקָּבֵר
Where you die, I will die, and there I will be buried

No one can really tell anyone else what the meaning of his life should be. This is just as well; only a puppet could be so instructed. It is the very essence of human existence to search for this personal meaning to one's personal existence, to formulate it, and to discover it. It is the very essence of life's adventure and man's creativity. It may even be that, while the meaning of one man's life is something very tangible and definite, that of another is the search for it. It is told of Rabbi Israel Baal Shem Tov that, lying on his deathbed, he was heard to say: "Now I know what I have lived for."

As far as a Jew is concerned, despite the fact that he might often feel frustrated, depressed, or dejected at not being able to discover the

17 Where you die, I will die, and there I will be buried. Thus and more may the Lord do to me if anything but death parts me from you."

subjective, personal element within the meaning of his existence, his life can never be completely meaningless. For he shares with all other Jews in the objective meaningfulness to be found within the frame of reference of Torah.

Crisis and Faith, page 45

כֹּה יַעֲשֶׂה יְהוָה לִי וְכֹה יוֹסִיף כִּי הַמָּוֶת יַפְרִיד בֵּינִי וּבֵינֵךְ

Thus and more may the Lord do to me if anything but death parts me from you

That life itself is a fundamental value, that it should be defended even at the risk of losing it, need not be argued. That life is holy and that therefore it must not be destroyed but should be protected, is essential Jewish teaching. However, *Kiddush haChayim* is not just the acknowledgment of the holiness of life, but the deed of its sanctification. Life as such is given to man; its sanctification is the task of man. In what, then, does life's sanctification consist, and how does it relate to *Kiddush haShem*, the sanctification of "the Name"?

The sanctification of life is achieved through a certain kind of human conduct. We find an indication of its meaning in the biblical injunction, "Thou shalt be holy, for I the Eternal your God am holy" (Leviticus 19:1, see the entire chapter, as well as chapter 20). Holiness derives then from Israel's relationship to God and from the awareness that God is holy. The laws that follow this introductory injunction describe the behavior that is the sanctification of life, comprising responsibilities toward God and toward one's fellow men. Other laws of the Torah, all aiming at the sanctification of life, include legislation concerning man's behavior in nature towards all creation. Sanctification of life means living in the world with the awareness that all life is God's creation and all life is living in His presence. Seeing the world as God's creation excludes the possibility of seeing spirit and matter as antagonistic to each other. The stance of the hero who, in the face of death, proves the "spirit's contempt for the flesh" would be heresy in Judaism. The flesh is no less God's creation than the spirit, and the spirit, as God's creation, is no less real than the flesh. Together they are life within man, and not only within man, but in all creation. According to a midrash, at the time of

יחוַתֵּרֶא כִּי־מִתְאַמֶּצֶת הִיא לָלֶכֶת אִתָּהּ וַתֶּחְדַּל לְדַבֵּר אֵלֶיהָ:
יטוַתֵּלַכְנָה שְׁתֵּיהֶם עַד־בֹּאָנָה בֵּית לָחֶם וַיְהִי כְּבוֹאָנָה בֵּית לֶחֶם וַתֵּהֹם
כָּל־הָעִיר עֲלֵיהֶן וַתֹּאמַרְנָה הֲזֹאת נָעֳמִי: כוַתֹּאמֶר אֲלֵיהֶן אַל־תִּקְרֶאנָה לִי
נָעֳמִי קְרֶאןָ לִי מָרָא כִּי־הֵמַר שַׁדַּי לִי מְאֹד:

---

creation God used the Torah as the blueprint for the world (Midrash
Rabbah, Bereishit 1:2). This, of course, is not meant to be taken literally.
Rather it expresses an important Jewish idea about the nature of reality.
Creation, as a work of God, cannot be alien to the Torah as the word
of God for man. Both make manifest the will and wisdom of God vis-
à-vis man. One might perhaps say that the sanctification of life means
living in the presence of God, striving for integrated harmonization of
spirit and flesh as the wholeness of human life, and giving this striving
potent expression in responsible human behavior towards all creation.

With God in Hell, pages 104–105

how determined she was to go with her   כִּי־מִתְאַמֶּצֶת הִיא לָלֶכֶת אִתָּהּ

The concept of authenticity of being was introduced into modern exis-
tentialist philosophy by Martin Heidegger. He meant by this the form
of human existence that is not determined by external conditions and
whose values do not derive from "them," from the standard bearers of
the established social order in the midst of which a human being may
find himself. Jean-Paul Sartre developed the thought further when he
spoke of freedom as a condition to which man is "condemned," meaning that no matter in what situation a person may find himself, he is
always free to make his choices and, indeed, he always does choose
between different possibilities of behavior. The decision is always his.
When the Gestapo tortured a member of the Maquis to get him to
betray his comrades, he was still free to choose to die or to reveal. His
betrayal might be understandable; it is not a matter of condemning
him. But in all circumstances, the decision is his.

Sartre's position is no mere theory. His understanding of human
freedom is based on his actual experiences in the French underground.
Similarly, Viktor Frankl, basing himself on his observations in the concentration camps, affirms the reality of human freedom even in extreme
conditions. He writes: "The experiences of camp life show that man

[18] When [Naomi] saw **how determined she was to go with her**, she ceased to argue with her; [19] and the two went on until they reached Bethlehem. When they arrived in Bethlehem, the whole city buzzed with excitement over them. The women said, "Can this be Naomi?" [20] "Do not call me Naomi," she replied. "**Call me Mara, for Shaddai has made my lot very bitter**.

---

does have a choice of action… Man can preserve a vestige of spiritual freedom, of independence of mind, even in such terrible conditions of psychic and physical stress." There were always choices to make, and it was your decision that "determined whether you would or would not submit to those powers which threatened to rob you of your very self, your inner freedom…"

For the Jew, there is no surprise in these discoveries of Sartre and Frankl. He has made his choices all through history and the Jewish people have survived to this day because there were always Jews who knew that no matter what the conditions and circumstances, it was always up to them to make the decision. We are not only thinking of the untold martyrs who made their choice, in the supreme freedom of the spirit, to die rather than to surrender, but also – and perhaps chiefly – of the ordinary daily life of the Jewish masses through the ages. They lived in confrontation with cultures and civilizations whose values they often rejected and whose lifestyles they mostly did not share. The Jew has been the nonconformist of history and has lived in the authenticity of selfhood through many centuries.

With God in Hell, pages 61–62

קְרֶאןָ לִי מָרָא כִּי־הֵמַר שַׁדַּי לִי מְאֹד

Call me Mara, for Shaddai has made my lot very bitter

Interpreting the words of the psalmist: "I pour out my complaint before Him, I declare before Him my trouble" (Psalms 142:3), the Midrash remarks: "Thus the men of faith declare their troubles before God" (Midrash Tehillim). In all their simplicity, these few words, which seem to add nothing to the text, are among the deepest observations on the essence of prayer. To pour out one's heart before God means simply to tell God about one's troubles. To pray means to make God the confidant of one's sorrow and need. The asking and begging are natural enough, but

כֹּא**אֲנִי֙ מְלֵאָ֣ה הָלַ֔כְתִּי וְרֵיקָ֖ם הֱשִׁיבַ֣נִי יְהֹוָ֑ה לָ֣מָּה תִקְרֶ֧אנָה לִ֣י נׇעֳמִ֗י וַֽיהֹוָה֙ עָ֣נָה בִ֔י וְשַׁדַּ֖י הֵרַ֥ע לִֽי׃**

---

they are of secondary importance. Decisive is the pouring of the heart because one has to; We pour out our hearts before God because He is the nearest, because He is the closest because He is the natural confidant of the human soul. All asking is in reality self-seeking; whether we ask for bread or health, for the power to do good, or "the enjoyment of God," we are asking for ourselves, for the things that we desire. "Give, give!" is no prayer, no matter what we ask for. We may ask only if we pray – if the request comes without premeditation in the wake of the cry. Our asking may have the quality of prayer, if it issues from the act of intimacy, of having made God our confidant.

Prayer, pages 28–29

אֲנִי֙ מְלֵאָ֣ה הָלַ֔כְתִּי וְרֵיקָ֖ם הֱשִׁיבַ֣נִי יְהֹוָ֑ה
I went away full, and the Lord has brought me back empty

Even though, on the one hand, one was never to despair, the requirements of the halacha did not allow Jews to forget the true nature of their situation. To trust in God does not mean fooling oneself regarding the prospects of tomorrow. According to talmudic teaching, those who escape from any dangerous situation or crisis should offer thanks to God by saying the blessing *Birchat haGomel*: "Blessed art Thou Eternal, our God, king of the universe, who renderest goodness to the guilty and hast rendered all good to me" (Brachot 54b). After one of the worst "selections," when thousands of Jews had been forcibly removed from a certain ghetto, the remaining community asked the following question. In view of the fact that they had escaped being selected and transported to the only too-well-known "unknown destination," were they obligated to recite the *Birchat haGomel*? The answer they received was in the negative for two reasons. Firstly, having escaped one "selection" was no real escape. In essence, the danger had not passed and might reoccur at any time. Secondly, reciting a thanksgiving blessing for having been saved would lull the people into a false sense of security. Thus, it was ruled that the situation did not warrant the recitation of the blessing (Ephraim Oshry, *She'elot uTshuvot MiMa'amakim*, Volume 1, Chapter 7).

With God in Hell, pages 35–36

²¹ I went away full, and the Lord has brought me back empty. How can you call me Naomi, when the Lord has dealt harshly with me, **when Shaddai has brought misfortune upon me!**"

---

when Shaddai has brought misfortune upon me   וְשַׁדַּי הֵרַע לִי

All through history, the greatest Jews have confronted God with the same problems that have been raised, with justifiable passion, by this post-Holocaust generation. Thus, for instance, the prophet Habakkuk (1:13):

> "Thou that art of eyes too pure to behold evil,
> And that canst look on mischief,
> Wherefore lookest Thou, when they deal treacherously,
> And holdest Thy peace, when the wicked swalloweth up
> The man that is more righteous than he?"

We may recall the words of Jeremiah (12:1), too, questioning the justice of divine providence:

> "Right wouldest Thou be, O Eternal,
> Were I to contend with Thee,
> Yet will I reason with Thee:
> Wherefore does the way of the wicked prosper?
> Wherefore are all they secure that deal very treacherously?"

The classical biblical discussion of this theme is found, of course, in the book of Job. The undeserved suffering of the innocent is the basis of the most severe questioning of God's ways with men. It is not a little surprising that God Himself approves of Job's contending with him.

In the Talmud, too, there is a full realization that the question of divine justice presents the Jew with a very serious problem. It is expressed in the terse formula: "A righteous man and it is ill with him; a wicked one and he does well." צדיק ורע לו, רשע וטוב לו (See the discussions in Ta'anit 11a and Kiddushin 39b). Elisha ben Avuyah became a heretic because of this problem and was known thereafter as *acher*, "the changed one." He looms large in the pages of the Talmud and forces upon the conscience of Judaism the awareness of the seriousness of this issue.

כבוַתָּשָׁב נָעֳמִי וְרוּת הַמּוֹאֲבִיָּה כַלָּתָהּ עִמָּהּ הַשָּׁבָה מִשְּׂדֵי מוֹאָב וְהֵמָּה
בָּאוּ בֵּית לֶחֶם בִּתְחִלַּת קְצִיר שְׂעֹרִים:

פרק ב

וּלְנָעֳמִי (מידע) מוֹדָע לְאִישָׁהּ אִישׁ גִּבּוֹר חַיִל מִמִּשְׁפַּחַת אֱלִימֶלֶךְ

The teachers of the Talmud took painful notice of God's many silences
in history at times when his manifestation in the affairs of men was
most anxiously awaited. Thus, for instance, the words of the Psalmist:
"Who is a mighty one, like unto Thee, O Eternal" were explained in the
following way: "Who is so mighty and strong as Thou, able to listen to
the blasphemy and insult of that wicked man (in this particular case,
Titus) and yet remain silent" (Gittin 56b).

It is worth noting that while it is not too difficult to find solutions
for the problems of reason, it is doubtful that they greatly influence the
condition of faith. The believer usually proves to himself what he had
already accepted prior to the finding of the solutions and the non-be-
liever remains, mostly, "unconvinced." The existential questions, however, usually raise great passions and lead to strong accusations against
God. Nevertheless, the faith of the questioner often remains unaffected
despite Heaven's silence. Neither Habakkuk nor Jeremiah was ever
given an answer. Job was, in a sense, silenced by divine omnipotence
with his questions still unanswered, and yet he was at peace. And so it
was in the ghettos and the camps, the questions were asked, even rebel-
liously, and though there were no answers, in the midst of questioning,
faith remained alive.

With God in Hell, pages 117–119

וַתָּשָׁב נָעֳמִי וְרוּת הַמּוֹאֲבִיָּה כַלָּתָהּ עִמָּהּ הַשָּׁבָה מִשְּׂדֵי מוֹאָב

**And Naomi and Ruth the Moabite, her daughter-in-law, returned
with her, from the country of Moab**

It is, however, quite obvious that the Jewish people can no longer continue as before. The God of history Himself has acknowledged this
fundamental truth of the problematics of Jewish existence by guiding
the Jews back to the land of their fathers, in His own mysterious way.

22 And Naomi and Ruth the Moabite, her daughter-in-law, returned from the country of Moab. They arrived in Bethlehem at the beginning of the barley harvest.

CHAPTER 2

Now Naomi had a kinsman on her husband's side, **a man of substance**, of the family of Elimelech, whose name was Boaz. ²Ruth

---

In the light of our latest experience of what man is capable of doing to his fellow, and in view of the present international cynicism and general erosion of human conscience, and the supreme modern technological efficiency of mass murder, we must not lose sight of the ever-present possibility of another disaster similar to the one that overtook the Jewish people during the Second World War.

Never again may we be caught unprepared. Before anything else, this ought to mean the return of Jews from all over the world to the land of Israel in their masses.

With God in Hell, pages 154–155

a man of substance   אִישׁ גִּבּוֹר חַיִל

The comradeship of David and Jonathan was lasting because it was "Love that did not depend on a Thing." And the same dictum continues: "Whenever Love depends on a Thing, with the passing of that Thing, Love too passes away; but when Love is not dependent on a Thing, it will not pass away forever" (Mishna Avot 5:16).

What is this "Thing" on which so much stress is laid in this saying of our masters, upon which so often Love does depend and upon which Love should not be dependent?

The Thing refers to social status, business and profession, money, and material success. The Thing is not the person, it is not the man. And this is not self-evident. Unfortunately, there is great need for stressing this point, for the Thing is very often mistakenly thought of as the person. In times of peace a man is judged not so much by what he is as by what he has. The Thing, be it money or social influence, position, or possession – the Thing, which one holds in his grasp, determines the status of a man on earth. In our civilization, too much depends on the

וְשָׁמוֹ בֹּעַז: בּוַתֹּאמֶר רוּת הַמּוֹאֲבִיָּה אֶל־נָעֳמִי אֵלְכָה־נָּא הַשָּׂדֶה וַאֲלַקֳטָה
בַשִּׁבֳּלִים אַחַר אֲשֶׁר אֶמְצָא־חֵן בְּעֵינָיו וַתֹּאמֶר לָהּ לְכִי בִתִּי: גוַתֵּלֶךְ
וַתָּבוֹא וַתְּלַקֵּט בַּשָּׂדֶה אַחֲרֵי הַקֹּצְרִים וַיִּקֶר מִקְרֶהָ חֶלְקַת הַשָּׂדֶה לְבֹעַז
אֲשֶׁר מִמִּשְׁפַּחַת אֱלִימֶלֶךְ: דוְהִנֵּה־בֹעַז בָּא מִבֵּית לֶחֶם וַיֹּאמֶר לַקּוֹצְרִים

Thing, too little on the person. A man is clever if he has success; he is respected if he holds office; he is trusted if he possesses securities. We have too much faith in the Thing, too little in character and personality.

It is the Thing that determines human relationships too. People associate in families, societies, and organizations – so we believe. In reality, however, it is one social status that associates with another of the same level, one group of interests with another, one bank account with another bank account of a similar weight and importance; in short – one Thing with another, but not one man with his fellow men. We have built up the power of the Thing. We believed that the more of it we held in our grip the more powerful we would be. And now the Thing dominates us. It counts more than man himself. Friendship, love, honor, and influence are today all dependent on the Thing, on what a man has and not on what he is. The Thing has enslaved man.

The Thing stands between man and man, it separates nation from nation. Thanks to ingenious inventions, distances are continually shrinking in our days; the distance between one man and another does not diminish. It happens very seldom that man meets man, that one heart turns to another, that one mind reveals itself to another, that one person associates with another person. The Thing stands between us and renders understanding between human beings almost impossible. Our associations of friendship and love are seldom lasting; they depend too much on the respect in which we hold the Thing and too little on the appreciation of the human personality.

Comradeship, however, is different. It emerges in circumstances in which nothing else counts but the man, and in which everything depends on character and courage, reliability, and faithfulness. Out there

the Moabite said to Naomi, "I would like to go to the fields and glean among the ears of grain, behind someone who shows favor in your eyes." "Yes, daughter, go," she replied; ³and off she went. She came and gleaned in a field, behind the reapers; and, **as luck would have it**, it was the piece of land belonging to Boaz, who was of Elimelech's family. ⁴And behold, Boaz came from Bethlehem and said to the

in the trenches, a man is judged by what he is and not by what he has. There the power of the Thing, the false magic of material possession and material success is broken. There, especially in the hour of danger, man meets man. Out of this meeting, a lasting understanding arises that may well be called: Love independent of the Thing. In comradeship, the dignity of man triumphs over the enslaving power of the Thing.

But comradeship should not be limited to service men only. It is a message of the front line to the world. It is a program for mankind. Today I feel that the world is better prepared to accept the message and the program than at any other moment in the history of man.

Between Yesterday and Tomorrow, pages 133–134

as luck would have it   וַיִּקֶר מִקְרֶהָ

Since all events in the world occur under the iron law of causality, it is maintained that any answer to prayer, which would bring about a result that otherwise might not be expected, would require a direct interference on the part of God with the laws of nature. Every prayer would be asking for a miracle. We fully appreciate that one may well be able to believe in the possibility of miracles and yet should reject the idea of a divine response to prayer which would constitute an interference with the laws of nature. What would indeed become of any orderliness in nature if, in response to the unceasing supplication of the human race, God would continually interfere with the natural course of events? The result would probably be like pushing the world back into the original *Tohu Va'Vohu*.

Prayer, page 88

יְהֹוָה עִמָּכֶם וַיֹּאמְרוּ לוֹ יְבָרֶכְךָ יְהֹוָה: הֹוַיֹּאמֶר בֹּעַז לְנַעֲרוֹ הַנִּצָּב עַל־
הַקּוֹצְרִים לְמִי הַנַּעֲרָה הַזֹּאת: יֹוַיַּעַן הַנַּעַר הַנִּצָּב עַל־הַקּוֹצְרִים וַיֹּאמַר
נַעֲרָה מוֹאֲבִיָּה הִיא הַשָּׁבָה עִם־נָעֳמִי מִשְּׂדֵי מוֹאָב: יֹוַתֹּאמֶר אֲלַקֳטָה־נָּא
וְאָסַפְתִּי בָעֳמָרִים אַחֲרֵי הַקּוֹצְרִים וַתָּבוֹא וַתַּעֲמוֹד מֵאָז הַבֹּקֶר וְעַד־עַתָּה
זֶה שִׁבְתָּהּ הַבַּיִת מְעָט: יֹוַיֹּאמֶר בֹּעַז אֶל־רוּת הֲלוֹא שָׁמַעַתְּ בִּתִּי אַל־
תֵּלְכִי לִלְקֹט בְּשָׂדֶה אַחֵר וְגַם לֹא תַעֲבוּרִי מִזֶּה וְכֹה תִדְבָּקִין עִם־נַעֲרֹתָי:
טֹעֵינַיִךְ בַּשָּׂדֶה אֲשֶׁר־יִקְצֹרוּן וְהָלַכְתְּ אַחֲרֵיהֶן הֲלוֹא צִוִּיתִי אֶת־הַנְּעָרִים
לְבִלְתִּי נָגְעֵךְ וְצָמִת וְהָלַכְתְּ אֶל־הַכֵּלִים וְשָׁתִית מֵאֲשֶׁר יִשְׁאֲבוּן הַנְּעָרִים:
יֹוַתִּפֹּל עַל־פָּנֶיהָ וַתִּשְׁתַּחוּ אָרְצָה וַתֹּאמֶר אֵלָיו מַדּוּעַ מָצָאתִי חֵן בְּעֵינֶיךָ

God be with you   יְהֹוָה עִמָּכֶם

"It is time to act for God" (Tehillim 119:126) applies not only in matters directly connected with divine service, like the preservation of the
Temple of Jerusalem. At times, it is permitted to suspend a biblical
law even by an action whose purpose is altogether social. We read in a
mishna: "It was established [by the sages] that one should greet one's
fellow man with the name of God. For thus we read in the Bible: 'And
behold, Boaz came from Bethlehem and said to the harvesters: God
be with you.'" This practice, reintroduced in mishnaic times, was not at
all self-evident. According to the Torah, one must not take the name
of God in vain. To justify this form of greeting, the mishna quotes the
verse, "It is time to act for God," which one of its teachers, R. Natan,
interprets: "Dissolve the law in order to act for God" (Brachot 54a). In
this instance, the explanation of Rashi is most revealing. He writes: "At
times one abolishes the words of the Torah in order to act for God. So
this one, too, whose concern is with the well-being of his fellow man, is
doing the will of God. For it is written, 'Seek peace and pursue it.' It is
permissible to dissolve the Torah and do what appears to be forbidden."

To some extent, this is an exceptional case of "it is time to act for
God." There is no real suspension of any law here. Because of a divine

harvesters, "**God be with you**!" And they responded, "The Lord bless you!" ⁵ Boaz said to the servant who was in charge of the reapers, "Whose girl is that?" ⁶ The servant in charge of the reapers replied, "She is a Moabite girl who came back with Naomi from the country of Moab. ⁷ She said, 'Please let me glean and gather among the sheaves behind the reapers.' **She has been on her feet ever since she came this morning**. She has rested but little in the hut." ⁸ Boaz said to Ruth, "Listen to me, daughter. Don't go to glean in another field. Don't go elsewhere, but stay here close to my girls. ⁹ Keep your eyes on the field they are reaping, and follow them. I have ordered the men not to molest you. And when you are thirsty, go to the jars and drink some of [the water] that the men have drawn." ¹⁰ She prostrated herself with her face to the ground, and said to him, "Why have I found

commandment, "Seek peace and pursue it," (Tehillim 34:15) one is actually urged to greet his neighbor with the Divine Name. Far from taking this name in vain, one actually does the will of God.

Not in Heaven, pages 100–101

וַתָּבוֹא וַתַּעֲמוֹד מֵאָז הַבֹּקֶר

She has been on her feet ever since she came this morning

In my home in Rumania, we had a village girl working for us as a servant. In the morning, she would clean the shoes of the family, she would set the table and, of course, put a jug full of water on it. Occasionally, as would be the case with children, we would dirty our shoes during the day, but we were not permitted to ask the maid to clean them again for us. During the day, if we wanted clean shoes, we had to clean them ourselves. When during a meal the water bottle would be emptied, the maid might have been asked by the lady of the house to bring another jug of water to the table, but we children were not allowed to ask her to bring a glass of water especially for us. Our father explained: the maid has certain duties in this house. She works and she is paid for her work, but she is not the personal servant of anyone in the house.

Crisis and Faith, pages 116–117

לְהַכִּירֵנִי **וְאָנֹכִי נָכְרִיָּה**: יֹּ וַיַּעַן בֹּעַז וַיֹּאמֶר לָהּ הֻגֵּד הֻגַּד לִי כָּל־אֲשֶׁר־
עָשִׂית אֶת־חֲמוֹתֵךְ אַחֲרֵי מוֹת אִישֵׁךְ וַתַּעַזְבִי אָבִיךְ וְאִמֵּךְ וְאֶרֶץ מֽוֹלַדְתֵּךְ
וַתֵּלְכִי אֶל־עַם אֲשֶׁר לֹא־יָדַעַתְּ תְּמוֹל שִׁלְשׁוֹם: יבּ יְשַׁלֵּם יְהֹוָה פָּעֳלֵךְ וּתְהִי

---

when I am a foreigner   וְאָנֹכִי נָכְרִיָּה

In the Talmud, there are a large number of terms for non-Jews, such
as gentile – a stranger (*Nochri – Zar*), *Goy* – nation (son of a different
nation), Samaritan – a dweller in Kuta, *Akum* – star-worshiper (an ac-
ronym for worshipers of the stars and constellations). To any intelligent
person, it is clear that one cannot substitute one appellation for another
at random. But it seems that today it is nearly impossible to find anyone
who can define the exact differences and possible nuances between the
various names. The lack of clarity on this issue increased due to the cen-
sorship in the Talmud, and lead to complete confusion. They changed
the terms "gentile" and "stranger" (*Nochri – Zar*) and "Goy" indiscrim-
inately for "*Akum*" or "Samaritan" with the intention of removing from
the Talmud any unpleasant reference which could perhaps be applied to
Christians as well. (Using the terms "gentile" (*Nochri*), "stranger" (*Zar*)
or "*Goy*" it would be possible to include the Christians, but it would not
be possible if they used the term "Samaritan" – a son of the city Kuta, or
"*Akum*" – a star-worshiper. This was the rationale of the censors.)

The term gentile – stranger (*Nochri*) presupposes the existence of
a Jewish State or an autonomous Jewish society. The gentile (*Nochri)*
is one who does not live permanently in such an autonomous Jewish
society, and whose laws do not apply to him. That is, not the gentile
himself, but more precisely: the "stranger" [a son of another country]
the non-Jew. (See Deuteronomy 29:21, "And the stranger (*Nochri*) who
comes from a far-off land…"

What is the Talmud, VIII, 2 (Sefaria.org)

favor in your eyes to single me out, **when I am a foreigner**?" [11] Boaz said in reply, "I have been told of all that you did for your mother-in-law after the death of your husband, how you left your father and mother and the land of your birth **and came to a people** you had not known before. [12] May the Lord reward your deeds. May you have

---

and came to a people   וַתֵּלְכִי אֶל־עַם

Judaism is not a religion of individual souls but that of a people. This again is due to the fact that Judaism is not a creed in the sense that one should be saved by faith alone; in Judaism, one must implement one's belief and one's deeds. The deed, however, is life in its entirety, and life in its entirety is never life in isolation, not even that of the individual. The whole of life, in all its manifestations – personal or political, ethical or economical, individual or social – must be lived with the awareness that it is being enacted by man in the presence of God. This is not a task for an individual, but for mankind as a whole; and until such time when mankind, as a whole, may embrace the responsibility, it will be realizable only by "a smaller mankind," a people that is committed to the aspiration of living its life as a people in the Sight of God. One may believe in Judaism as an individual, one can live as a Jew only together with other Jews. It is in this sense that Judaism is the religion of a people. It is the way of life of a whole people; it is the way of life that has determined the essential quality of a people. In Judaism it is not only the individual that confronts God; the people, as a people, is committed to living in such confrontation. As it lives as a people in the presence of God so it turns to God in prayer as a people. This is specifically Jewish. *T'filat Tsibbur* is not congregational prayer; every *Minyan* is an *Eidah*, because it signifies the whole of Israel. Jews assembled in prayer are not a congregation but a miniature national assembly at prayer.

Prayer, page 55

מַשְׂכֻּרְתֵּ֗ךְ שְׁלֵמָ֔ה מֵעִ֛ם יְהֹוָ֥ה אֱלֹהֵ֖י יִשְׂרָאֵ֑ל אֲשֶׁר־בָּ֖את לַחֲס֥וֹת תַּֽחַת־
כְּנָפָֽיו׃ ֡יוַתֹּ֗אמֶר אֶמְצָא־חֵ֤ן בְּעֵינֶ֙יךָ֙ אֲדֹנִ֔י כִּ֥י נִֽחַמְתָּ֖נִי וְכִ֥י דִבַּ֙רְתָּ֙ עַל־לֵ֣ב
שִׁפְחָתֶ֔ךָ וְאָנֹכִי֙ לֹ֣א אֶֽהְיֶ֔ה כְּאַחַ֖ת שִׁפְחֹתֶֽיךָ׃ ֡ידוַיֹּ֩אמֶר֩ לָ֨ה בֹ֜עַז לְעֵ֣ת הָאֹ֗כֶל
גֹּ֤שִֽׁי הֲלֹם֙ וְאָכַ֣לְתְּ מִן־הַלֶּ֔חֶם וְטָבַ֥לְתְּ פִּתֵּ֖ךְ בַּחֹ֑מֶץ וַתֵּ֙שֶׁב֙ מִצַּ֣ד הַקּֽוֹצְרִ֔ים
וַיִּצְבׇּט־לָ֣הּ קָלִ֔י וַתֹּ֥אכַל וַתִּשְׂבַּ֖ע וַתֹּתַֽר׃ ֡טווַתָּ֖קׇם לְלַקֵּ֑ט וַיְצַו֩ בֹּ֨עַז אֶת־

יְהֹוָה֙ אֱלֹהֵי֙ יִשְׂרָאֵ֔ל אֲשֶׁר־בָּ֖את לַחֲס֥וֹת תַּֽחַת־כְּנָפָֽיו
the God of Israel, under whose wings you have sought refuge

Knowledge of God means that the whole system possesses only one fundamental belief, the belief in a personal God. Everything else is knowledge, i.e., it is either logically derived from the basic idea of the personal God, or revealed in history. (The thirteen "*Ikkarim*" (Dogmas) of Maimonides are no credo, they represent a theological disputation with other religious systems.) And the Way of God is the way that men should walk as a logical outcome of their belief in God. Although it is impossible to define it in a few words, it probably comes nearest to the truth to say that Judaism is not a "religion" but a Way of Living based upon the belief in a Personal God. The idea that a Personal God should lead to the Way of Living, is perfectly logical. For a Personal God means a personally ever-present God; a God continually looking on, continually looking at you. It means that life is always and everywhere; it is life in the presence of God. The conception of life given by God and to be lived in the perennial presence of God must inescapably lead to a definite way of living. For God is looking on to see, and in giving us life He has given us the chance to show what we are. God's Eyes, watching us, render life always and everywhere the God-given testing ground of men. Wherever we are, whatever we do, we are being tested and watched. This is the situation with which man is confronted as long as he lives. The conception of life as the inescapable testing ground of man demands a Way of Living that embraces the whole of life, every branch of it, every moment of it; a way that must be signalized by an awareness of the eternal Divine Presence and by the endeavor of man to stand that test always and everywhere without relaxing for one moment.

Towards Historic Judaism, pages 70–71

a full recompense from the Lord, **the God of Israel, under whose wings you have sought refuge!**" [13] She answered, "**I have found favor in your eyes my lord, to comfort me and to speak gently to the heart, to your maidservant** – though I am not so much as one of your maidservants." [14] At mealtime, Boaz said to her, "Come over here and partake of the meal, and dip your morsel in the vinegar." So she sat down beside the reapers. He handed her roasted grain, and she ate her fill and had some left over. [15] When she got up again to glean, Boaz gave orders to his workers, "You are not only to let her

---

אֶמְצָא־חֵן בְּעֵינֶיךָ אֲדֹנִי כִּי נִחַמְתָּנִי וְכִי דִבַּרְתָּ עַל־לֵב שִׁפְחָתֶךָ

I have found favor in your eyes my lord, to comfort me and to speak gently to the heart, to your maidservant

---

Let an example from my own personal experience show what I mean by the right approach to our fellow Jews. One Erev Shabbat, a distinguished orthodox rabbi in Chicago asked me to see a young girl, who was in town for the weekend with her father. The father was desperate. He had come from afar to spend some time with his daughter, who was staying at a Christian missionary school in the area. The rabbi thought that I was the right person to see the girl since her problem was a matter of theology and religious philosophy. I saw her on a Saturday night. She came with her father. She was all Christian piety and lovingkindness. Her natural loveliness and vitality were completely subdued into calm and simplicity worthy of a nun. She was a young girl who, like so many of the young people of that generation, had been "into" everything. Finally, she had converted to Christianity and was chosen to be educated as a missionary. After the social preliminaries in the company of the family were over, we retired into my study. I realized soon enough that my task was not to talk theology to her, or to prove to her the superiority of Judaism over Christianity. Before anything else, I had to understand her. We talked, or rather I let her talk, encouraging her to continue, to go on, occasionally asking a question, making a remark. Finally, after about three hours, when I thought I understood her, I said to her quietly: "You have been hurt, badly hurt." At which she started crying. After that everything went relatively easily; after that we could talk about Judaism and Christianity, about being a Jew, about almost any other subject under the sun. She stayed with us for a

נְעָרָיו לֵאמֹר גַּם בֵּין הָעֳמָרִים תְּלַקֵּט וְלֹא תַכְלִימְוּהָ: ‏ט״ז‏ וְגַם שֹׁל־תָּשֹׁלּוּ
לָהּ מִן־הַצְּבָתִים וַעֲזַבְתֶּם וְלִקְּטָה וְלֹא תִגְעֲרוּ־בָהּ: ‏י״ז‏ וַתְּלַקֵּט בַּשָּׂדֶה
עַד־הָעָרֶב וַתַּחְבֹּט אֵת אֲשֶׁר־לִקֵּטָה וַיְהִי כְּאֵיפָה שְׂעֹרִים: ‏י״ח‏ וַתִּשָּׂא וַתָּבוֹא
הָעִיר וַתֵּרֶא חֲמוֹתָהּ אֵת אֲשֶׁר־לִקֵּטָה וַתּוֹצֵא וַתִּתֶּן־לָהּ אֵת אֲשֶׁר־הוֹתִרָה
מִשָּׂבְעָהּ: ‏י״ט‏ וַתֹּאמֶר לָהּ חֲמוֹתָהּ אֵיפֹה לִקַּטְתְּ הַיּוֹם וְאָנָה עָשִׂית יְהִי מַכִּירֵךְ
בָּרוּךְ וַתַּגֵּד לַחֲמוֹתָהּ אֵת אֲשֶׁר־עָשְׂתָה עִמּוֹ וַתֹּאמֶר שֵׁם הָאִישׁ אֲשֶׁר עָשִׂיתִי
עִמּוֹ הַיּוֹם בֹּעַז: ‏כ׳‏ וַתֹּאמֶר נָעֳמִי לְכַלָּתָהּ בָּרוּךְ הוּא לַיהוָֹה אֲשֶׁר לֹא־
עָזַב חַסְדּוֹ אֶת־הַחַיִּים וְאֶת־הַמֵּתִים וַתֹּאמֶר לָהּ נָעֳמִי קָרוֹב לָנוּ הָאִישׁ

---

few weeks. Then she went home with her father, returned to her people and to its faith. The experience also changed the life of the entire family, who became *Shomrei Mitzvot*, Torah-observant Jews.

As we try to provide for the spiritual hunger of our day, before anything else we must try to understand, to act with kindness, and brotherly love. If we wish to offer guidance to the perplexed, we can only do it if we forever bear in mind that all of them, without distinction, *Keru'im banim lashem*, are called God's children. We can only meet the challenge and respond to the opportunities of these times with faith in *Am Yisrael*, in the promise hidden in every Jewish soul.

Crisis and Faith, pages 172–173

וְגַם שֹׁל־תָּשֹׁלּוּ לָהּ מִן־הַצְּבָתִים וַעֲזַבְתֶּם וְלִקְּטָה

but you must also pull some [stalks] out of the heaps and leave them for her to glean

---

Once again, there was no written code to consult. On the basis of the rabbis' understanding of the overriding Torah-purpose formulated nowhere explicitly, but absorbed into their own consciousness as the result of a life of dedication and commitment to Torah and its living realization, they gave the answer, a halachic solution to a halachic problem.

The examples are innumerable. For instance, the case of Rabba bar Bar Hana who had hired some workers to carry some barrels of wine. Somehow, the workers broke the barrels and the wine was lost. Whereupon Rabba took away their clothes as a guarantee for, or in lieu of, damages, to which he thought he was entitled. They brought the case for adjudication before Rab, who ruled that the clothes were to be re-

glean among the sheaves, without interference, [16] **but you must also pull some [stalks] out of the heaps and leave them for her to glean**, and not scold her." [17] She gleaned in the field until evening. Then she beat out what she had gleaned – it was about an 'ephah of barley – [18] and carried it back with her to the town. When her mother-in-law saw what she had gleaned, and when she also took out and gave her what she had left over after eating her fill, [19] her mother-in-law asked her, "Where did you glean today? Where did you work? Blessed be he who took such generous notice of you!" So she told her mother-in-law whom she had worked with, saying, "The name of the man with whom I worked today is Boaz." [20] Naomi said to her daughter-in-law, "**Blessed be he of the Lord, who has not failed in His kindness to the living or to the dead**!" For, Naomi explained to her

---

turned to the workers. Asked Rabba: "Is this the law?" And the answer was: "Yes! for it is written, 'That you walk in the way of good men.'" The clothes were returned. The workers, however, were not yet satisfied. "We have worked all day and we are hungry," they said, claiming their wages. Rab ruled: "Go and pay them their wages." Once again Rabba asked: "Is this the law?" and the answer was given: "Yes! For the verse in Proverbs concludes: 'And keep the paths of the righteous.' (Baba Metziah 83a)" Legalistically speaking, Rabba, of course, was right. Such was not the law. But the case before Rab presented one of those characteristically halachic problems. There was the law of damages. But there was also the obligation to care for the disadvantaged. Once again, the decision was made on the basis of a rabbi's appreciation of the more comprehensive concern of the Torah. Rab's decision was not in accordance with the specific law of damages, but with the total purpose of the Law of the Torah. It was halacha.

Crisis and Faith, pages 87–88

בָּרוּךְ הוּא לַיהוָה אֲשֶׁר לֹא־עָזַב חַסְדּוֹ אֶת־הַחַיִּים וְאֶת־הַמֵּתִים

Blessed be He of the Lord, who has not failed in His kindness to the living or to the dead

---

Kant's God is great, but not great enough; therefore, one cannot pray to him. The One who is omniscient and omnipotent in such a manner that he can even bend down and lend an ear to the supplication of a poor

מְגֹאֲלֵנוּ הוּא: כֹּאוַתֹּאמֶר רוּת הַמּוֹאֲבִיָּה גַּם | כִּי־אָמַר אֵלַי עִם־הַנְּעָרִים אֲשֶׁר־לִי תִּדְבָּקִין עַד אִם־כִּלּוּ אֵת כָּל־הַקָּצִיר אֲשֶׁר־לִי: כֹּבוַתֹּאמֶר נָעֳמִי אֶל־רוּת כַּלָּתָהּ טוֹב בִּתִּי כִּי תֵצְאִי עִם־נַעֲרוֹתָיו וְלֹא יִפְגְּעוּ־בָךְ בְּשָׂדֶה אַחֵר: כֹּגוַתִּדְבַּק בְּנַעֲרוֹת בֹּעַז לְלַקֵּט עַד־כְּלוֹת קְצִיר־הַשְּׂעֹרִים וּקְצִיר הַחִטִּים וַתֵּשֶׁב אֶת־חֲמוֹתָהּ:

---

fool is greater. He alone is God. Is this a small matter in comparison with the universal plans of divine wisdom? The brilliance of the Milky Way may arouse us to admire the Creator; the power and wisdom that sustains the galaxies of immeasurable space may fill our hearts with awe and adoration. At every step, the magnificence of His works may be revealed to us in the smallest as well as the greatest of His creations. Unsurpassed in grandeur and majesty, however, is the fact that the One who wields all that power and wisdom is also the One who seeks out the company of man. That prayer is possible, that man can approach God because God desires to be approached by man, is the glory of all Divine glories. When the psalmist, looking up to the skies praised God in the words: "The heavens declare the glory of God, and the firmament showeth His handiwork" (Psalms 19:1), he took cognizance of the plans of Divine omnipotence and omniscience. Yet, he was able to conclude the psalm so begun with the prayer, so often recited by Jews, "Let the words of my mouth and the meditation of my heart be acceptable to Thee, O Eternal One, my Rock and my Redeemer" (Psalms 19:14). He could do so because he knew that those very plans of omnipotence and omniscience were only part of God's more universal plan of infinite mercy. It is within that plan that prayer has its due place.

Prayer, pages 77–78

לְלַקֵּט עַד־כְּלוֹת קְצִיר־הַשְּׂעֹרִים וּקְצִיר הַחִטִּים

and gleaned until the barley harvest and the wheat harvest were finished

---

In a rather surprising passage, the prophet Isaiah describes the implications of mishpat in the labors of the plowman (28:23–29).

daughter-in-law, "the man is related to us; he is one of our redeeming kinsmen." [21] Ruth the Moabite said, "He even told me, 'Stay close by my workers until all my harvest is finished.'" [22] And Naomi answered her daughter-in-law Ruth, "It is best, daughter, that you go out with his girls, and not be annoyed in some other field." [23] So she stayed close to the maidservants of Boaz, **and gleaned until the barley harvest and the wheat harvest were finished**. Then she stayed at home with her mother-in-law.

Give ye ear, and hear my voice;
Attend, and hear my speech.
Is the plowman never done with plowing to sow,
With the opening and harrowing of his ground?
When he hath made plain the face thereof,
Doth he not cast abroad the black cumin, and scatter the cumin,
And put in the wheat in rows and the barley in the appointed place
And the spelt in the border thereof?
For He doth instruct him to *mishpat*;
His God doth teach him.
For the black cumin is not threshed with a threshing-sledge,
Neither is a cart-wheel turned about upon the cumin;
But the black cumin is beaten out with a staff,
And the cumin with a rod.
Is bread corn crushed?
Nay, he will not ever be threshing it;
And though the roller of his wagon and its sharp edges move noisily,
He doth not crush it.
This also cometh forth from the Lord of hosts:
Wonderful is His counsel, and great His wisdom.

The *mishpat*, which God teaches the plowman is not essentially different from the one by which, measuring and weighing the various parts of his creation, he establishes their relationship to each other and makes the universe an enduring and functioning entity. It is the same *mishpat* of relatedness and balance, applied to the corner of the world in

פרק ג

וַתֹּאמֶר לָהּ נָעֳמִי חֲמוֹתָהּ בִּתִּי הֲלֹא אֲבַקֶּשׁ־לָךְ מָנוֹחַ אֲשֶׁר יִיטַב־לָךְ: בּוְעַתָּה הֲלֹא בֹעַז מֹדַעְתָּנוּ אֲשֶׁר הָיִית אֶת־נַעֲרוֹתָיו הִנֵּה־הוּא זֹרֶה אֶת־גֹּרֶן הַשְּׂעֹרִים הַלָּיְלָה: גוְרָחַצְתְּ ׀ וָסַכְתְּ וְשַׂמְתְּ (שמלתך) שִׂמְלֹתַיִךְ עָלַיִךְ (וירדתי) וְיָרַדְתְּ הַגֹּרֶן אַל־תִּוָּדְעִי לָאִישׁ עַד כַּלֹּתוֹ לֶאֱכֹל וְלִשְׁתּוֹת: דוִיהִי בְשָׁכְבוֹ וְיָדַעַתְּ אֶת־הַמָּקוֹם אֲשֶׁר יִשְׁכַּב־שָׁם וּבָאת וְגִלִּית מַרְגְּלֹתָיו (ושכבתי) וְשָׁכָבְתְּ וְהוּא יַגִּיד לָךְ אֵת אֲשֶׁר תַּעֲשִׂין: הוַתֹּאמֶר אֵלֶיהָ כֹּל אֲשֶׁר־תֹּאמְרִי אֵלַי (קרי ולא כתיב) אֶעֱשֶׂה: ווַתֵּרֶד הַגֹּרֶן וַתַּעַשׂ כְּכֹל אֲשֶׁר־צִוַּתָּה חֲמוֹתָהּ: זוַיֹּאכַל בֹּעַז וַיֵּשְׁתְּ וַיִּיטַב לִבּוֹ וַיָּבֹא לִשְׁכַּב בִּקְצֵה הָעֲרֵמָה וַתָּבֹא בַלָּט וַתְּגַל מַרְגְּלֹתָיו וַתִּשְׁכָּב: חוַיְהִי בַּחֲצִי הַלַּיְלָה וַיֶּחֱרַד הָאִישׁ וַיִּלָּפֵת

---

which the plowman performs his task. How the earth is to be plowed, how the various seeds are to be sown in relationship to each other, how each of the seeds is to be treated after having yielded the hoped-for harvest, all must be done according to a *mishpat* which is from God and which, like the original comprehensive, universal *mishpat*, reveals God's wonderful counsel and wisdom. But why was it so important for the prophet to draw the attention of the people to the *mishpat* that the plowman has to obey? Surely, he was not lecturing to them on the art of agriculture. The point he was making was that *mishpat* is a universal principle. It prevails everywhere, in the realm of the spirit no less than in the realm of nature. As there is an orderliness, appropriateness, and balanced relatedness of all things in nature without which life is not possible, so is there also the same kind of *mishpat* in all matters of the spirit.

Man and God, pages 243–245

CHAPTER 3

Naomi, her mother-in-law, said to her, "Daughter, I must seek calmness for you, where it is beneficial to you. ² Now there is our kinsman Boaz, whose girls you were close to. He will be winnowing barley on the threshing floor tonight. ³ So bathe, anoint yourself, dress up, and go down to the threshing floor. But do not disclose yourself to the man until he has finished eating and drinking. ⁴ When he lies down, note the place where he lies down, and go over and uncover his feet and lie down. He will tell you what you are to do." ⁵ She replied, "**I will do everything you tell me**." ⁶ She went down to the threshing floor and did just as her mother-in-law had instructed her. ⁷ Boaz ate and drank, and in a cheerful mood went to lie down beside the grain pile. Then she went over stealthily and uncovered his feet and lay down. ⁸ In the middle of the night, the man gave a start

---

I will do everything you tell me   כֹּל אֲשֶׁר־תֹּאמְרִי אֵלַי אֶעֱשֶׂה

Judaism does not encourage proselytism because the proselyte accepts a great many duties and responsibilities which previously were not incumbent upon him and concerning which, therefore, he could never lose his "innocence." A Gentile, who does not practice Judaism, is not a sinner; a proselyte, by becoming a Jew, exposes himself to the wider possibilities of failure and sin. At the same time, Judaism looks with admiration and respect on the "Ger Tsedek," the "Righteous Proselyte," who becomes a Jew out of inner conviction. His prototype is the Patriarch Abraham, who found his way to God by free choice and personal faith. The proselyte of conviction is "beloved by God," he is "great in the sight of God," for he becomes a Jew for the sake of God. "Happy is every one that feareth the Lord, that walketh in His ways": the verse is applied to him (See Talmud, Gerim, 4:3, Midrash Rabba, Bamidbar, 8:2 and 9).

Judaism; Fossil or Ferment, page 68

וְהִנֵּה אִשָּׁה שֹׁכֶבֶת מַרְגְּלֹתָיו: ‏ יּ‏וַיֹּאמֶר מִי־אָתְּ וַתֹּאמֶר אָנֹכִי רוּת אֲמָתֶךָ
וּפָרַשְׂתָּ כְנָפֶךָ עַל־אֲמָתְךָ כִּי גֹאֵל אָתָּה: ‏ יּ‏וַיֹּאמֶר בְּרוּכָה אַתְּ לַיהֹוָה בִּתִּי

וַיֹּאמֶר מִי־אָתְּ וַתֹּאמֶר אָנֹכִי רוּת אֲמָתֶךָ וּפָרַשְׂתָּ כְנָפֶךָ עַל־אֲמָתְךָ

"Who are you?" he asked. And she replied, "I am your handmaid
Ruth. Spread your garb over your handmaid

The Talmud tells the story of a man who was extremely careful in the
observance of the commandment of *tzitzit*, of wearing ritual fringes on
the four corners of one's garb. Once he heard that there was a prostitute
in a city by the sea whose fee was four hundred gold pieces. He sent
her the four hundred gold pieces and a time was arranged for him.
When the day arrived, he went to the door of her house. Her maid
went in and told her: "That man who sent you the four hundred pieces
of gold has come and sits at the door." Said she: "Let him enter." He
entered. She had prepared for him seven beds, six of silver and one of
gold. They were arranged one above the other and between each there
was a ladder made of silver. The highest bed was the one of gold. She
climbed up to the top and lay down naked in the golden bed. Then he
too climbed up to sit down opposite her in the nude. At this moment
the *tzitziyot*, the four fringes of his garb, came and slapped him across
the face. At this, he broke away and sat down on the ground. She too
came down and sat on the ground. Said she to him: "By the Capitol of
Rome! I shall not let you off until you tell me what blemish you saw in
me." Said he to her: "I swear I have never seen a woman as beautiful as
you, but there is a commandment that God commanded us, its name
is *tzitzit*. The words in which they are written contain the phrase, 'I am
the Lord your God' twice, meaning: I am the one who calls to account;
I am the one who will reward. Now, they (the *tzitzit*) appeared to me as
if they were four witnesses." Said she to him: "I shall not let you off till
you tell me your name, the name of your city, of your rabbi, the name of
the school where you study Torah." He wrote it all down and placed it
into her hand. Then she got up and divided all her property into three
parts: a third for the government, a third for the poor, and a third she
took with her, apart from "that bed linen" (which was not included in

and pulled back – there was a woman lying at his feet! [9] **"Who are you?" he asked. And she replied, "I am your handmaid Ruth. Spread your garb over your handmaid**, for you are a redeeming kinsman." [10] He exclaimed, **"Be blessed of the Lord, daughter!**

---

the division). She proceeded to the study house of Rabbi Ḥiyya and said to him: "Rabbi! Command that I be made a convert." Said he to her: "My daughter, is it perhaps that one of the students appealed to your eyes?" She took the note (that he had given her) from her hand and gave it to him. Whereupon (after reading it) he said to her: "Go and take possession of what you have acquired." The story concludes with this moral: And so the same bed linen that she once spread out for him to serve his lust, she now spread out for him in consecrated union. This was the reward for the *mitzvah* of *tzitzit* in this world. How much in the world to come, who can tell (Menachot 44a).

Crisis and Faith, pages 64–66

Be blessed of the Lord, daughter!　　　　בְּרוּכָה אַתְּ לַיהוָֹה בִּתִּי

There is one more aspect to this story (in Menachot 44a.) Though redeemed from his lust, the man is fully open to the woman's beauty. She, on the other hand, does not hide the fact that she desires the man, but the whole man, in his bio-psychic completeness. The story ends with a statement of the sensual enjoyment of their union, that is seen as this-worldly reward for the careful observance of the *mitzvah* that protects a man against going astray after his "heart" and his "eyes."

This story contains all the basic principles of Jewish sex ethics. It recognizes the force of the sexual instinct while illustrating how this instinct in its impersonal givenness depersonalizes a human being. It need not be repressed. Indeed, it can be raised to the personal level of human existence as the natural outcome of the personalization of the relationship between a man and a woman who encounter each other in the completeness of their bio-psychic being. Finally, as in our earlier systematic presentation, so in the story too, personalization is twofold. It is accomplished between the Jew and his God, and between the man and the woman. Thus they are rejoicing together in the presence of God.

הֵיטַבְתְּ חַסְדֵּךְ הָאַחֲרוֹן מִן־הָרִאשׁוֹן לְבִלְתִּי־לֶכֶת אַחֲרֵי הַבַּחוּרִים אִם־
דַּל וְאִם־עָשִׁיר: יֹּוְעַתָּה בִּתִּי אַל־תִּירְאִי כֹּל אֲשֶׁר־תֹּאמְרִי אֶעֱשֶׂה־לָּךְ כִּי
יוֹדֵעַ כָּל־שַׁעַר עַמִּי כִּי אֵשֶׁת חַיִל אָתְּ: יֹּבוְעַתָּה כִּי אָמְנָם כִּי (אם כתיב ולא
קרי) גֹאֵל אָנֹכִי וְגַם יֵשׁ גֹּאֵל קָרוֹב מִמֶּנִּי: יֹּלִינִי הַלַּיְלָה וְהָיָה בַבֹּקֶר אִם־
יִגְאָלֵךְ טוֹב יִגְאָל וְאִם־לֹא יַחְפֹּץ לְגָאֳלֵךְ וּגְאַלְתִּיךְ אָנֹכִי חַי־יְהֹוָה שִׁכְבִי
עַד־הַבֹּקֶר: יֹּדוַתִּשְׁכַּב מַרְגְּלוֹתָו עַד־הַבֹּקֶר וַתָּקָם בְּטֶרֶם (בטרום) יַכִּיר
אִישׁ אֶת־רֵעֵהוּ וַיֹּאמֶר אַל־יִוָּדַע כִּי־בָאָה הָאִשָּׁה הַגֹּרֶן: יֹּווַיֹּאמֶר הָבִי

Once redeemed from the bondage of the impersonal, neither the eye
nor the heart has to be denied. They lead, but do not lead astray.

Crisis and Faith, page 70

הֵיטַבְתְּ חַסְדֵּךְ הָאַחֲרוֹן מִן־הָרִאשׁוֹן
Your latest deed of kindness is greater than the first

God's way with his creation is God's law for his creation. God's law
for man emanates from God's way with man. All law is God's way,
appropriately reflected in the realm of human existence. All biblical
law, in a sense, is *imitatio dei*. To practice *chesed* and *rachamim*, which is
a way for God, thus itself is God's law for man. This is in keeping with
the numerous passages in the Bible which require of man that he keep
or do lovingkindness, compassion, and charity.

Man and God, page 242

---

as the Lord lives חַי־יְהֹוָה

For the person who does not recognize the presence of God in the Exodus, at Sinai, in the words of the prophets, or in innumerable events of
Jewish history, Auschwitz presents no problem of faith. For him, God
is forever absent. Only the Jew who has known of the presence of God
is baffled and confounded by Auschwitz. What conclusions is he to
draw from this terrifying absence of divine concern? Is God indifferent
to human destiny? But the Jew knows otherwise. He knows of the
most intimate divine concern. Has God, perhaps, died? Is it possible
that once upon a time there was a God who was not indifferent toward
Israel, but that now something has happened to Him, He has gone

Your latest deed of kindness is greater than the first, in that you have not turned to younger men, whether poor or rich. [11] And now, daughter, have no fear. I will do on your behalf whatever you ask, for all the elders of my town know what a fine woman you are. [12] But while it is true I am a redeeming kinsman, there is another redeemer closer than I. [13] Stay for the night. Then in the morning, if he will act as a redeemer, good! let him redeem. But if he does not want to act as redeemer for you, I will do so myself, **as the Lord lives**! Lie down until morning." [14] So she lay at his feet until dawn. **She rose before one person could distinguish another**, for he thought,

---

away, and He is no longer? This is plain silly. It is possible for a human being to lose faith in God. But it is not possible for God to die. He either is and therefore, will ever be; or He is not and, therefore never was. But if God was, is, and will ever be, is it possible that at Auschwitz He rejected Israel and turned away from Israel as a punishment for its sins? To believe this would be a desecration of the Divine Name. No matter what the sins of European Jewry might have been, they were human failings. If the holocaust was a punishment, it was a thousandfold inhuman. The only crime of man for which such punishment might be conceivable would be the Nazi crime of Germany, and even there, one would hesitate to impose it.

Faith After the Holocaust, pages 138–139

וַתָּקָם בְּטֶרֶם יַכִּיר אִישׁ אֶת־רֵעֵהוּ

She rose before one person could distinguish another

Rabbi Leo Baeck, rabbi of the liberal Berlin Jewish community and, under the Nazi regime, head of the Reichsvertretung Deutscher Juden, tells that the Jews in the camp were well aware of the fact that any day, any hour, they might face death. No one could know when the murderers would pick them up for "selection." Yet Jews did not sit and weep. They revealed super-human steadfastness by secretly assembling in the darkness of night in order to study Torah, participate in courses on Jewish subjects, and listen to lectures on eternal questions, the mysteries of existence beyond the reach of human understanding. Not only did the participants endanger their lives in case of possible discovery by the Germans, but there was also the added health risk. All day

הַמִּטְפַּחַת אֲשֶׁר־עָלַיִךְ וְאֶחֳזִי־בָהּ וַתֹּאחֶז בָּהּ וַיָּמָד שֵׁשׁ־שְׂעֹרִים֙ וַיָּשֶׁת עָלֶיהָ
וַיָּבֹא הָעִיר: ט"וַתָּבוֹא אֶל־חֲמוֹתָהּ וַתֹּאמֶר מִי־אַתְּ בִּתִּי וַתַּגֶּד־לָהּ אֵת כָּל־
אֲשֶׁר עָשָׂה־לָהּ הָאִישׁ: י"וַתֹּאמֶר שֵׁשׁ־הַשְּׂעֹרִים הָאֵלֶּה נָתַן לִי כִּי אָמַר אֵלַי
(קרי ולא כתיב) אַל־תָּבוֹאִי רֵיקָם אֶל־חֲמוֹתֵךְ: י"חַוַתֹּאמֶר שְׁבִי בִתִּי עַד
אֲשֶׁר תֵּדְעִין אֵיךְ יִפֹּל דָּבָר כִּי לֹא יִשְׁקֹט הָאִישׁ כִּי־אִם־כִּלָּה הַדָּבָר הַיּוֹם:

פרק ד

וּבֹעַז עָלָה הַשַּׁעַר֙ וַיֵּשֶׁב שָׁם֙ וְהִנֵּה הַגֹּאֵל עֹבֵר֙ אֲשֶׁר דִּבֶּר־בֹּעַז וַיֹּאמֶר
סוּרָה שְׁבָה־פֹּה פְּלֹנִי אַלְמֹנִי וַיָּסַר וַיֵּשֵׁב: ב"וַיִּקַּח עֲשָׂרָה אֲנָשִׁים מִזִּקְנֵי
הָעִיר וַיֹּאמֶר שְׁבוּ־פֹה וַיֵּשֵׁבוּ: ג"וַיֹּאמֶר֙ לַגֹּאֵל חֶלְקַת הַשָּׂדֶה אֲשֶׁר לְאָחִינוּ

---

the prisoners were subjected to grinding slave labor, after which they needed rest above all in order to recover. However, the truth was that these "spiritual injections," as Dr. Baeck calls them, the courses and the homilies, far from weakening these Jews, actually strengthened them, revived them, and gave them new energies to endure the cruelties of the camp.

"I shall never forget these meetings," wrote Dr. Baeck. "We would assemble in pitch darkness. To light a candle or even a match would have brought immediate disaster upon all of us. Nevertheless, in the midst of all that darkness, I sensed light. The faces of these Jews were illuminated by an unearthly radiance, as one was talking to them about matters of the spirit and the eternal questions, about God, about Jews and the world, about the eternity of Israel. I sensed a light in that darkness, the light of the Torah." His listeners would assure the rabbi that the study and the lectures not only strengthened them spiritually but even their physical stamina was improved by them. "I often contemplated my people," concludes Dr. Baeck, "their faces I could not distinguish, but I saw great light."

With God in Hell, pages 11–12

"Let it not be known that the woman came to the threshing floor."
¹⁵ And he said, "Hold out the shawl you are wearing." She held it
while he measured out six measures of barley, and he put it on her
back. When she got back to the town, ¹⁶ she came to her mother-in-
law, who asked, "How is it with you, daughter?" She told her all that
the man had done for her; ¹⁷ and she added, "He gave me these six
measures of barley, saying to me, 'Do not go back to your mother-
in-law empty-handed.'" ¹⁸ And Naomi said, "Stay here, daughter, till
you learn how the matter turns out. For the man will not rest, but
will settle the matter today."

CHAPTER 4

Meanwhile, Boaz had gone to the gate and sat down there. And now
the redeemer whom Boaz had mentioned passed by. He called, "Come
over and sit down here, So-and-so!" And he came over and sat down.
² Then [Boaz] took **ten elders of the town** and said, "Be seated here";

| ten elders of the town | עֲשָׂרָה אֲנָשִׁים מִזִּקְנֵי הָעִיר |

There remains just one more point that requires elucidation, the principle that "every sacred service requires a minyan," a quorum of ten
male participants. First, we must bear in mind that this is not a biblical
command. Noting that the reciting of the *Shema* is undoubtedly a *da-
var she-bi-ḳedushah* (sacred prayer), Rabbenu Jonah tells us that there
is nothing in our prayers more sacred than the words expressing our
acceptance of the yoke of God's rule, yet the *Shema* does not require
a quorum of ten and may well be recited individually. Therefore, the
phrase "every sacred service" cannot be taken literally.

The meaning of the principle can only be that every prayer that was
originally instituted as requiring ten people must be so observed. Since
the recitation of the *Shema* was never so established, it may be recited
in private even though it is holier than the other prayers that have the
character of *ḳedushah* (holiness). One may, however, ask: If the requirement of the quorum of ten was originally instituted by the rabbis, how
are we to understand the talmudic explanation that the rule is derived
from a verse in the Torah, "And I shall be sanctified in the midst of the

לֶאֱלִימֶלֶךְ מָכְרָה נָעֳמִי הַשָּׁבָה מִשְּׂדֵה מוֹאָב: דוַאֲנִי אָמַרְתִּי אֶגְלֶה אָזְנְךָ
לֵאמֹר קְנֵה נֶגֶד הַיֹּשְׁבִים וְנֶגֶד זִקְנֵי עַמִּי אִם־תִּגְאַל גְּאָל וְאִם־לֹא יִגְאַל
הַגִּידָה לִּי (וְאֵדַע) וְאֵדְעָה כִּי אֵין זוּלָתְךָ לִגְאוֹל וְאָנֹכִי אַחֲרֶיךָ וַיֹּאמֶר אָנֹכִי
אֶגְאָל: יוַיֹּאמֶר בֹּעַז בְּיוֹם־קְנוֹתְךָ הַשָּׂדֶה מִיַּד נָעֳמִי וּמֵאֵת רוּת הַמּוֹאֲבִיָּה
אֵשֶׁת־הַמֵּת (קָנִיתִי) קָנִיתָ לְהָקִים שֵׁם־הַמֵּת עַל־נַחֲלָתוֹ: יוַיֹּאמֶר הַגֹּאֵל

---

children of Israel," (Leviticus 22:32) interpreting "in the midst" as in the midst of a minimum of ten?

Undoubtedly the derivation from the Bible is not to be taken literally. First of all, the various daily services are not a biblical command but a rabbinical *takkanah* (arrangement). Secondly, the biblical words "And I shall be sanctified in the midst of the children of Israel" require *Kiddush haShem* (the sanctification of the Divine Name by sacrificing oneself even if one's life is threatened, rather than deny God in public). Now, this command has nothing to do with prayer services, nor does it discriminate between men and women. In the given situation, all Jews are obligated to *Kiddush haShem* (sanctification of the Divine Name). This verse in the Bible, stating that one needs a public quorum of at least ten in order to recite some of the more sacred parts of the prayer service, like the *Kedushah* and *Barchu*, is used as what is known as an *asmakhta*, a borrowed biblical verse on which a rabbinical institution "leans" for support. But then, of course, one may ask whence the basis for the determination that only men may form a minyan. The original meaning of the biblical support does not distinguish between male and female children of Israel. The fact is that nowhere in the Talmud where the quorum of ten is mentioned is it stated that the ten must all be men. The exclusion of women from the communal service can only be another rabbinical arrangement added to the first rabbinical *takkanah* of public prayer with ten members. What might have been the reason for this additional requirement for which the biblical verse cannot be used even as an *asmakhta*, a borrowed support? Quite clearly, it could not have been that women lack the purity needed. As we saw, the *Shema* is a more sacred prayer than any of the parts of the daily prayer for which a *minyan* of ten males is required, yet it is prayed even in private by men and women alike. The reason for the exclusion of women from the

and they sat down. ³He said to the redeemer, "Naomi, now returned from the country of Moab, must sell the piece of land which belonged to our kinsman Elimelech. ⁴I thought I should disclose the matter to you and say: Acquire it in the presence of those seated here and in the presence of the elders of my people. If you are willing to redeem it, redeem! But if you will not redeem, tell me, that I may know. For there is no one to redeem but you, and I come after you." "I am willing to redeem it," he replied. ⁵Boaz continued, "When you acquire the property from Naomi and from Ruth the Moabite, **you must also acquire the wife of the deceased**, so as to perpetuate the name of

─────────────────────────────────

tefillah be-tzibbur (communal prayer) can only be that the rabbis would not allow men and women to pray together. If that is so, one might give serious consideration to the halachic possibility of a female *minyan*, i.e., of allowing the recitation of *Kedushah* and *Barchu* at women's prayers services in the presence of a minimum of ten women.

Jewish Women in Time and Torah, pages 92–93

you must also acquire the wife of the deceased   אֵשֶׁת־הַמֵּת קָנִיתָ

No one knows how many problems arose, and how much human suffering, in the years soon after the European tragedy of the Jewish people. Let one post-Holocaust personal experience, but morally quite disturbing, illustrate the point. I was a rabbi in Sydney, Australia. One day, a couple came to my office. The woman was a concentration-camp survivor. She had lost everything. Her entire family had been wiped out. She had been married but had no children. Her husband, too, had been murdered. She was alone in the world. Through correspondence, she had discovered that a friend of hers from her hometown had managed to get to Australia. She came to Australia to marry him. But... her late husband once had a brother. What had become of him, no one knew. Was he alive somewhere, or had he too been murdered? If he was still alive, the woman needed *halitza* before she could remarry.

What was the rabbi to do? Institute an international search for witnesses? And in the meantime? Hadn't she suffered enough, not a personal fate but the fate of all Israel? Finally, she had found someone willing to build a new home with her, to start a new life. What was to

לֹא אוּכַל֙ (לגאול) לִגְאָל־לִ֔י פֶּן־אַשְׁחִ֖ית אֶת־נַחֲלָתִ֑י גְּאַל־לְךָ֤ אַתָּה֙ אֶת־
גְּאֻלָּתִ֔י כִּ֥י לֹא־אוּכַ֖ל לִגְאֹֽל: וְזֹאת֩ לְפָנִ֨ים בְּיִשְׂרָאֵ֜ל עַל־הַגְּאֻלָּ֤ה וְעַל־
הַתְּמוּרָה֙ לְקַיֵּ֣ם כָּל־דָּבָ֔ר שָׁלַ֥ף אִ֛ישׁ נַעֲל֖וֹ וְנָתַ֣ן לְרֵעֵ֑הוּ וְזֹ֥את הַתְּעוּדָ֖ה

---

be her situation in the meantime, till all the inquiries were made and all the answers received? What if a brother-in-law were found alive in some distant land? Establish contact with him. Would he be willing or able to come to Australia for the *halitza*, or would she have to leave the promised shores of her hope in order to participate in the ceremony? Meanwhile, would she have to be placed in some kind of halachic quarantine, remaining homeless and awaiting happiness? By God, this was not what the Torah meant! This was not halacha; certainly not "ways of pleasantness and paths of peace"!

The tragic aspect of the present situation is that all the problems we have discussed in this section, and related ones, can be solved. In my halachic work *Conditionality in Marriage and Divorce*, I have shown that by including proper safeguards in the terms of the marriage contract, such predicaments can be eliminated *ab initio*. The practice of our time in the application of the Torah's marriage and divorce laws often leads to grievous human suffering and much desecration of God's name. It is ethically indefensible, but halacha is not responsible for it.

Not in Heaven, pages 159–160

Now this was formerly done in Israel וְזֹאת לְפָנִים בְּיִשְׂרָאֵל

It is a fundamental principle in Judaism that *Torat Mosheh* is unchangeable, eternal. But it is not part of Jewish doctrine to believe that the application of Torah to one special period of Jewish history must remain unalterably valid for all time. This would be illogical. The application of Torah to a certain situation can only remain valid as long as the situation remains unchanged. In fact, in the Talmud itself, authoritative decisions of a previous age are often rejected on the grounds that the situation has become different from that originally envisaged. The new application of the Torah does not mean rejection of the traditional one,

the deceased upon his estate." [6] The redeemer replied, "Then I cannot redeem it for myself, lest I impair my own estate. You take over my right of redemption, for I am unable to exercise it." [7] **Now this was formerly done in Israel** in cases of redemption or exchange: to validate any transaction, one man would take off his sandal and hand it to the other. Such was the practice in Israel. [8] So when the redeemer

---

for it is always undertaken in accordance with the same principles that have determined the halacha during previous periods of Jewish history. The new application is not overriding: it continues where others, even of greater authority, left off. (In certain circumstances, however, according to the system of the halacha even overriding is possible.) It is a historic accident and certainly no part of the intrinsic nature of Judaism that for many centuries, especially since the conclusion of the Talmud, neither overruling nor new authoritative application has been possible. This restriction has been forced on us by circumstances, not by Judaism. This was *galut*, i.e., Judaism waiting and preserving itself for a new chance of total realization. But Judaism cannot go on waiting now that the chance presents itself for a very important part of our nation to liquidate *galut*. It cannot be "preserved," it must move, it must progress; it must take up the thread where it has been left off; it must utilize all the potentialities of development which are included in the system of halacha. We must apply Torah and not some formerly valid application of Torah to this new form of Jewish existence for which it was never intended. To make this possible we must transform the rigid authority of the Talmud back into the living authority of a national institution such as it was originally. This can only happen after we have, so to speak, given ourselves to the Talmud, so that it becomes again part of our cultural and religious existence. Only when Judaism has become the main spiritual force in us can it unfold itself through us. We must reconquer the Talmud before Judaism can be freed from its present rigidity and further development be made possible.

Towards Historic Judaism, pages 59–60

בְּיִשְׂרָאֵל: חַוַיֹּאמֶר הַגֹּאֵל לְבֹעַז קְנֵה־לָךְ וַיִּשְׁלֹף נַעֲלוֹ: טוַיֹּאמֶר בֹּעַז
לַזְּקֵנִים וְכָל־הָעָם עֵדִים אַתֶּם הַיּוֹם כִּי קָנִיתִי אֶת־כָּל־אֲשֶׁר לֶאֱלִימֶלֶךְ
וְאֵת כָּל־אֲשֶׁר לְכִלְיוֹן וּמַחְלוֹן מִיַּד נָעֳמִי: יוְגַם אֶת־רוּת הַמֹּאֲבִיָּה אֵשֶׁת

---

he drew off his sandal וַיִּשְׁלֹף נַעֲלוֹ

This interpretation reflects the talmudic understanding that the Torah does not command anything that man, because of his intrinsic nature or the prevailing conditions, would not be able to do. This realization is the basis of a ramified series of *halachot*. According to the Torah, one must not marry the divorced wife or the widow of a brother. But if a man dies without offspring, it is a biblical commandment for his brother to marry the widow, so that through the building of a new family the name of the deceased brother may be preserved. This is known as *yibum*, or levirate marriage. If, however, the brother refuses to marry the widow, the ceremony of *halitza* is necessary, by which the woman is freed to marry whomever she pleases. According to this rule, the levirate marriage takes precedence over the *halitza* separation.

Nevertheless, during the mishnaic period, the rabbis reversed the order, arguing that *halitza* is preferred (Bechorot 13a). What was the reason for this? The explanation given is as follows: As a rule, a man must not marry the former wife of his brother; an exception, however, was made in the case of a brother who died without leaving children. In such a case, one fulfills a divine commandment by marrying the widow, in order to raise a family that will be considered as if it were that of the deceased brother. However, it was found that most people who would marry the widow would not do so for the sake of the *mitzvah*, in order to serve the name of a brother. People usually marry for personal reasons, because of attraction or other personal interests. Given human nature as the rabbis knew it, the biblical commandment was not realizable. Therefore, according to some commentaries, the levirate marriage was forbidden; according to others, it was only discouraged. According to to the one, a biblical law was abolished; according to the other, it was greatly reduced in meaning and importance.

To understand this, it is important to recall a talmudic principle:

said to Boaz, "Acquire for yourself," **he drew off his sandal**. [9] And Boaz said to the elders and to the rest of the people, "**You are witnesses today** that I am acquiring from Naomi all that belonged to Elimelech and all that belonged to Chilion and Mahlon. [10] Also of Ruth

---

"Where it is possible, it is possible; where it is not possible, it is not possible" (Chulin 11b). Let us look at some of the examples given. Assume an elderly or sick man lives away from his wife in a "land across the sea," a faraway country without the possibility of communication. He might be a man without children. If he should die, his wife will not be free to remarry whomever she wants, for the man has a brother, who may want to fulfill the commandment of the levirate marriage, or else will have to release her through the *halitza* ceremony. The husband wishes to relieve his wife from such dependence on a brother; therefore, he sends her a writ of divorce. It takes some time before the messenger arrives. In the meantime, the husband dies because of illness or old age. In such a case, the divorce ought to be invalid, for a divorce cannot take place after the husband's death. Nevertheless, the Mishna states that the messenger should hand the woman the writ under the assumption that the husband is alive. This accords with the halachic principle of *hazaka*, or presumption, according to which a condition, once established legally assumed to continue unchanged until the opposite becomes known.

Not in Heaven, pages 13–14

You are witnesses today · עֵדִים אַתֶּם הַיּוֹם

It is true that the exclusion of women from appearing as witnesses is based on a verse in the Torah (Shevuot 30a). However, there is a very important precedent for the acceptance of a woman as a judge – Deborah. Tosafot asks how Deborah could be a judge, since someone who is disqualified as a witness cannot be a judge (Bava Kama 15a). The answer given is: "Most likely she could function as a judge because the people accepted her on account of the *Shekhinah* (Divine Presence) that was with her." It is important to understand that it was not the presence of the *Shekhinah* that qualified her. The *Shekhinah* was the reason why the people accepted her and submitted to her authority. Her acceptance by the people was decisive. It was the people from whom she derived her authority.

מַחְלוֹן קָנִיתִי לִי לְאִשָּׁה לְהָקִים שֵׁם־הַמֵּת עַל־נַחֲלָתוֹ וְלֹא־יִכָּרֵת שֵׁם־הַמֵּת
מֵעִם אֶחָיו וּמִשַּׁעַר מְקוֹמוֹ עֵדִים אַתֶּם הַיּוֹם: יֹּאמְרוּ כָּל־הָעָם אֲשֶׁר־
בַּשַּׁעַר וְהַזְּקֵנִים עֵדִים יִתֵּן יְהֹוָה אֶת־הָאִשָּׁה הַבָּאָה אֶל־בֵּיתֶךָ כְּרָחֵל ׀
וּכְלֵאָה אֲשֶׁר בָּנוּ שְׁתֵּיהֶם אֶת־בֵּית יִשְׂרָאֵל וַעֲשֵׂה־חַיִל בְּאֶפְרָתָה וּקְרָא־

Such is, indeed, the halacha. People have the right to appoint someone as a judge over them or to trust him as a witness, even though
normally he would not be qualified for those tasks. A person has the
right to submit himself to an unqualified judge or witness. A father
cannot judge for a son, neither in his favor nor against him. Yet in a
case that requires legal judgment, if one party is willing to accept his
own father or the other party's father as a judge, then either father, as
the case may be, has the authority to function for the two parties as a
judge whose decision is binding. In fact, in many communities in which
courts were established to rule in matters of communal concern, it was
also customary, as a rule, to allow even relatives to testify in matters
of communal interest (Rashba, Responsa, 680). Not to admit women
as witnesses on the basis of their acceptance by the community of the
Jewish people would be to exclude them from the male world. However,
as we determined above, the principle of exclusion has lost its validity
in the phase of women's Torah-taught personal status. Indeed, in view
of women's share in social life and their role in it, the exclusively male
world does not exist any longer.

Jewish Women in Time and Torah, pages 77–78

I am acquiring as my wife   קָנִיתִי לִי לְאִשָּׁה

The binding formality of the marriage is the mutual acceptance of the
responsibility to persevere in the task of the full actualization of each
other's potential for the interpersonal life. It is a commitment to the
trust in that potential and as such an affirmation by innumerable daily
deeds of one's faith in the human being on the universal plane. The
formal marriage is not to be based on the present love that at this moment unites two human beings, but on the trust in the self-transcend-
ing power of that love, in its as-yet unfathomed potential that through

the Moabite, the wife of Mahlon, **I am acquiring as my wife**, so as to perpetuate the name of the deceased upon his estate, that the name of the deceased may not disappear from among his kinsmen and from the gate of his home town. You are witnesses today. [11] All the people at the gate and the elders answered, "We are. **May the Lord make the woman who is coming into your house like Rachel and Leah, both of whom built up the House of Israel!** Prosper in Ephrathah

---

care, devotion, and the practice of basic humanity and decency will carry two human beings to the richest bio-psychic fulfillment of which they are capable. However, just because personalization is the goal, the Jewish marriage does not include the commitment "till death do us part." Failure is always possible, mistakes are often made, and the relationship may degenerate into such an abysmal failure of impersonality that divorce may become a moral necessity.

Crisis and Faith, pages 75–76

יִתֵּן֩ יְהֹוָ֨ה אֶֽת־הָאִשָּׁ֜ה הַבָּאָ֣ה אֶל־בֵּיתֶ֗ךָ כְּרָחֵ֤ל ׀ וּכְלֵאָה֙ אֲשֶׁ֨ר בָּנ֤וּ שְׁתֵּיהֶם֙ אֶת־בֵּ֣ית יִשְׂרָאֵ֔ל

May the Lord make the woman who is coming into your house like Rachel and Leah, both of whom built up the House of Israel!

In addition to the legal status of the woman, a new concern that agitates many of us today is the religious status of the woman in the daily life of the Jewish community. This truly is a contemporary problem, resulting from radically changed intellectual, social, and economic conditions. The concern deals with what should be the place of the contemporary Torah-observant woman, who adheres to the rules of halacha, in the religious life of the community. Many of these women are well educated at colleges and universities and have a broad, and often highly specialized, secular education. Is it conceivable that they should continue to be excluded from any serious study of Torah and Talmud, and of the other disciplines in the study of Judaism, as they were in the past? What is bound to be the quality of Jewish life, in the homes and the communities, if intelligent, mentally alert women, otherwise fully involved in the moral, political, social, and economic issues of the day should be – as a matter of religious principle – relegated to the status of ignoramus within the realm where they ought to have their spiritual and religious roots, the realm of Judaism? Is the Jewish woman of today,

שֵׁם בְּבֵית לָחֶם: יֹּוִיהִי בֵיתְךָ֙ כְּבֵ֣ית פֶּ֔רֶץ אֲשֶׁר־יָלְדָ֥ה תָמָ֖ר לִֽיהוּדָ֑ה מִן־הַזֶּ֗רַע אֲשֶׁ֨ר יִתֵּ֤ן יְהֹוָה֙ לְךָ֔ מִן־הַנַּעֲרָ֖ה הַזֹּֽאת: יֹּוַיִּקַּ֨ח בֹּ֤עַז אֶת־רוּת֙

---

who intellectually, socially, and, often professionally too, is indeed the equal of her husband, to remain only a passive participant in the daily religious life of the community, often only the spectator to Judaism which, apparently, is essentially a male concern and responsibility?

Once again, we have reached a juncture at which the comprehensive ethos of the Torah itself strains against its formulation of specific laws. It is, however, the very essence of the halacha to be responsive to such a strain, and by its resolution to bring about an even richer realization of the Torah itself. Not only is the status of the woman at stake but the status of Judaism itself. For if in its application it could not do full justice to the Jewish woman in her present state as she is longing for participation in the drama of Jewish realization in accordance with her capacity and spiritual need, its form of such application becomes itself highly questionable. Those who understand the true nature and function of halacha, and are committed to halachic Judaism, cannot accept such a suggestion. With unreserved openness and sensitivity to the genuineness of the problem, with faith in the vitality of the halacha, with humility and yet with intellectual courage, the necessary halachic work will be accomplished that will define the status of the woman anew, justly and meaningfully.

Crisis and Faith, pages 120–121

וַיְהִי בֵיתְךָ֙ כְּבֵ֣ית פֶּ֔רֶץ אֲשֶׁר־יָלְדָ֥ה תָמָ֖ר לִֽיהוּדָ֑ה

And may your house be like the house of Perez whom Tamar bore to Judah

---

What then is *Kiddush haShem*, sanctification of God's name? The concept is charged with deep emotion for the Jew, as it carries within itself both the tragedy and the glory of Jewish martyrdom through the ages. It is with great hesitancy that one dares undertake even only a cursory discussion of this awesome subject. Because the idea of martyrdom has become so closely attached to it, *Kiddush haShem* is commonly un-

and perpetuate your name in Bethlehem! [12] **And may your house be like the house of Perez whom Tamar bore to Judah** – through the offspring which the Lord will give you by this young woman." [13] So Boaz married Ruth; she became his wife, and he cohabited with her.

derstood to mean dying a martyr's death as a Jew. But this does not appear to be its original meaning. For example, the phrase occurs in the talmudic interpretation of the biblical story of Tamar who, disguised as a prostitute, had been made pregnant by her father-in-law, Judah. Accused of harlotry by Judah, but not wanting to put him to shame, instead of naming him she sent him the pledges that he had left in her hands with the words: "I am pregnant by the man to whom these belong… Recognize, I pray thee, whose are these, the signet, and the cords, and the staff" (Genesis 38:25). The teachers in the Talmud considered the Hebrew *hakker na*, "recognize, I ask you," rather too strong a phrase for the identification of such objects as a signet, cords, and a staff. Usually, the root *hakker* (to recognize) in the Bible implies personal recognition. Therefore, here too, the midrashic interpretation attaches a personal form of acknowledgment to both phrases. Thus Tamar was asking Judah: "Please, acknowledge the presence of your Creator and do not hide your eyes from me." The Bible then continues: *Vayakker* Yehudah, "And Judah recognized." This phrase supports the midrashic interpretation for if the act of recognition referred to the objects before him, the syntax would have required the phrase: *Va'yakirem* Yehudah, "And Judah recognized them." As it stands, it is better rendered "And Judah acknowledged," i.e., acknowledged "the presence of his Creator" and confessed. By his acknowledgment, the Talmud says, Judah "sanctified the Divine Name." This deed of Judah is then compared to the conduct of Joseph who withstood temptation by the wife of Potiphar and thereby also "sanctified the Divine Name." Yet Judah's deed was greater than that of Joseph, for he performed the act of *Kiddush haShem* in public, whereas Joseph did so in private (Sotah 10b).

With God in Hell, pages 105–106

וַתְּהִי־לֹו לְאִשָּׁה וַיָּבֹא אֵלֶיהָ וַיִּתֵּן יְהֹוָה לָהּ הֵרָיֹון וַתֵּלֶד בֵּן: יד וַתֹּאמַרְנָה
הַנָּשִׁים אֶל־נָעֳמִי בָּרוּךְ יְהֹוָה אֲשֶׁר לֹא הִשְׁבִּית לָךְ גֹּאֵל הַיֹּום וְיִקָּרֵא
שְׁמֹו בְּיִשְׂרָאֵל: טו וְהָיָה לָךְ לְמֵשִׁיב נֶפֶשׁ וּלְכַלְכֵּל אֶת־שֵׂיבָתֵךְ כִּי כַלָּתֵךְ

The Lord let her conceive

וַיִּתֵּן יְהֹוָה לָהּ הֵרָיֹון

According to the Bible, a woman who gave birth brought a sacrifice to the Temple after the period of purification. If she could afford it, the sacrifice was a lamb "as a burnt offering" and a turtledove or pigeon "as a sin offering." If she was poor, she brought another dove or pigeon in place of the lamb (Leviticus 12:6,8). Now, if the woman failed to do this and had other births, she had to make offerings for each birth. For instance, after five births, she had to bring five such sacrifices. However, she did not have to bring them all at once. After the first sacrifice, she would be considered ritually pure again (meaning that she was permitted to partake of the meat of animals offered in the Temple). Apparently, women often neglected to offer the prescribed sacrifice after every birth, so their sacrificial obligations accumulated. Women owed three, four, five, or more such sacrifices. In accordance with the law of supply and demand, the price of pigeons usually went up. As the Mishna tells it:

> It happened once that the price for two such pigeons went up to a golden dinar. R. Shimon ben Gamliel, the head of the Sanhedrin, then took an oath and said: "I shall not go to bed tonight until the price goes down to a silver dinar.' He went into the study house and taught: "A woman, even if she gives birth five times, brings only one sacrifice; the rest are no obligation upon her." Soon after, the price of the pigeons came down to half a silver dinar (Kritot 8a).

Some of the commentaries are aghast. How could R. Shimon rule against the law? Rashi explains that even though R. Shimon was treating a biblical commandment lightly, it was an occasion "to act for the sake of God." The reference is to Psalms 119:126, "It is time for the eternal to work; they have violated your law," to which the rabbis gave the following midrashic interpretation: "At times one has to work for

The Lord let her conceive, and she bore a son. [14] And the women said to Naomi, "Blessed be the Lord, who has not withheld a redeemer from you today! **May his name be perpetuated in Israel**! [15] He

God by voiding his law." For if the prices did not go down, women would not bring even one sacrifice but would, nevertheless, eat of sacrificial meals in their ritual impurity. This was, indeed, one of these cases when one rules against the law for the sake of the law. But even Rashi, the great classical commentator on the plain meaning of all biblical and talmudic texts, was hesitant to accept the ruling of R. Shimon, as one may see from the fact that he had to give it a ritual justification – a reason for which there is not the slightest suggestion in the text. We are inclined to follow the view of Maimonides, who cites R. Shimon's declaration without any further comment (Maimonidies, *Mishne Torah*, Laws of Those Requiring Atoning Sacrifices 1:10). In this case, we have before us a perfect combination of economic and moral feasibility. Preventing the exploitation of the poor was indeed acting for the sake of God.

Not in Heaven, pages 27–28

May his name be perpetuated in Israel   וְיִקָּרֵא שְׁמוֹ בְּיִשְׂרָאֵל

Take for instance our times. Torah is forgotten in Anglo-Jewry. Of course, people may say that at least we have children. It is correct to say that we do bring children into the world. We love them and work for them; it is our great happiness to see them grow up and settle down. But once they have grown up, are they still ours? Do they still belong to us? Do we really have our children? They fight on all the fronts, except on the Jewish front. They give their hearts to many a cause but not to the Jewish cause. They are good youths. They are intelligent, idealistic and capable of enthusiasm but they are not ours. We do not have our children. Anglo-Jewry is gradually losing the battle for Jewish survival because it is losing its young. This, however, is the most natural thing on earth. A generation of Jews that is empty of Torah, of Jewish knowledge and culture, cannot and will not hold its youth. Children that ask and fathers who reply are not only a feature of the Seder evening but – and this is of far greater importance – also the foundation of Jewish life. The

אֲשֶׁר־אֲהֵבָתֶךְ֙ יְלָדַ֔תּוּ אֲשֶׁר־הִיא֙ ט֣וֹבָה לָ֔ךְ מִשִּׁבְעָ֖ה בָּנִֽים׃ ¹⁶וַתִּקַּ֨ח נָעֳמִ֤י
אֶת־הַיֶּ֙לֶד֙ וַתְּשִׁתֵ֣הוּ בְחֵיקָ֔הּ וַתְּהִי־ל֖וֹ לְאֹמֶֽנֶת׃ ¹⁷וַתִּקְרֶ֩אנָה֩ ל֨וֹ הַשְּׁכֵנ֥וֹת שֵׁם֙
לֵאמֹ֔ר יֻלַּד־בֵּ֖ן לְנָעֳמִ֑י וַתִּקְרֶ֤אנָה שְׁמוֹ֙ עוֹבֵ֔ד ה֥וּא אֲבִי־יִשַׁ֖י אֲבִ֥י דָוִֽד׃ {פ}

---

continued discussion between the generations depends on the future of
Judaism. But a child will not ask unless there is a father who can reply,
unless he can hope for guidance from his parents. We are losing our
youth because an ignorant Jewry has nothing to offer that our youth
deems worthwhile having.

Judaism is disintegrating from within thanks to the ambitious rule of
the *Am-ha'arets*. Assimilation is bad, Nazidom is worse; but worst of all
is the *Am-ha'arets* ruling and guiding Jewry. It is the end. The time has
come to declare a relentless war on Jewish ignorance. Let the voice of
Jacob be heard again within Jewry. Let children learn to ask and parents
to give answers, so that the great discussion between the generations
may continue. Let us have our children again that we may rely on them
to stand firm until a new day will dawn upon Israel.

Between Yesterday and Tomorrow, pages 122–123, 126

A son is born to Naomi   יֻלַּד־בֵּן לְנָעֳמִי

The conscious identification with the divine purpose of the life-propa-
gating cosmic principle is not simply the biological transmission of life
from generation to generation. This would still be an act of impersonality. As far as the Jew is concerned, the cosmic principle is personalized
when it is made to serve the transmission of the life of Judaism from

will renew your life and sustain your old age; for he is born of your daughter-in-law, who loves you and is better to you than seven sons." [16] Naomi took the child and held it to her bosom. She became its foster mother, [17] and the women neighbors gave him a name, saying, "**A son is born to Naomi**!" They named him Obed; he was the father of

generation to generation, What God had "spoken of Abraham" was never meant to be "brought upon him" in his own lifetime. It was to find its fulfillment in the course of the fullness of the bio-psychic history of all his children. Judaism is a process through history, beginning with Abraham, the father, moving towards its culmination in Abraham's child, the Messiah, when all history will be fully redeemed from the bondage of the impersonal. Because, in history, Judaism is forever striving for its realization, it is always lived with a sense of the "not yet." It is forever lived in the future and with responsibility toward that future. It is what it will yet be. A Jew, who desires to be one, is always a link in the generations, a child that receives and a parent that transmits with the intention and the freely accepted responsibility of furthering through time the bringing about at the end of time what God had "spoken of Abraham." Personalization of the union between a man and a woman is to be sought on the interpersonal level, in the presence of God, with the acceptance of responsibility for the historic destiny of all Israel. That is what Jewish ethics means by marriage and family. That is what we mean by the marriage formula: "Thou shalt be sanctified unto me according to the law of Moses and Israel."

Crisis and Faith, pages 77–78

יחוְאֵלֶּה תּוֹלְדוֹת פָּרֶץ פֶּרֶץ הוֹלִיד אֶת־חֶצְרוֹן: יטוְחֶצְרוֹן הוֹלִיד אֶת־
רָם וְרָם הוֹלִיד אֶת־עַמִּינָדָב: כוְעַמִּינָדָב הוֹלִיד אֶת־נַחְשׁוֹן וְנַחְשׁוֹן הוֹלִיד
אֶת־שַׂלְמָה: כאוְשַׂלְמוֹן הוֹלִיד אֶת־בֹּעַז וּבֹעַז הוֹלִיד אֶת־עוֹבֵד: כבוְעוֹבֵד
הוֹלִיד אֶת־יִשַׁי וְיִשַׁי הוֹלִיד אֶת־דָּוִד:

David   דָּוִד

When King David said, "I have set the Eternal One always before me"
(Psalms 16:8) he was of course not speaking of the specific occasions of
prayer. The word, "always" indicates that he was referring to something
that was going on continually. He had in mind his entire life, all the
activities of his everyday existence. All the time, he set the Eternal One
before him. The psalmist gave expression here to the very essence of
Jewish religiosity. Judaism implies the affirmation that God is forever
present, that all life is enacted in His sight. Therefore, it is man's responsibility to set this truth always before him; to live all the days of his life,
and to perform every one of his deeds with the awareness that it all
takes place in the presence of God. Only because of that is prayer possible in Judaism. Without it, the confrontation in prayer would indeed
be a mere "as if" situation. From the individual experience of God's

Jesse, father of David. [18] This is the line of Perez: Perez begot Hezron, [19] Hezron begot Ram, Ram begot Amminadab, [20] Amminadab begot Nahshon, Nahshon begot Salmon, [21] Salmon begot Boaz, Boaz begot Obed, [22] Obed begot Jesse, and Jesse begot **David**.

---

remoteness alone, one cannot step forward into the Presence and ask for the elimination of the distance. God is not present when man prays to Him; man may pray to Him because He is the always-present God. Out of the midst of the personal experience of God's hidden face, one faces God *as if* His face were not hidden from one. It is, indeed, an "as if" situation in relationship to one's personal experience; but it is not a situation of make-believe, for God is indeed always present and near. The confrontation may not always be subjectively real, yet it is objectively true. Only because it is objectively valid may, in the fulfillment of prayer, the "as if" confrontation ripen more and more into a personal experience of the Presence.

Prayer, page 13

יוֹם רִאשׁוֹן
קוֹרְאִים בְּחוּץ לָאָרֶץ וּבְאֶרֶץ יִשְׂרָאֵל

שְׁמוֹת יט:א–כ:כג; מַפְטִיר: בְּמִדְבַּר כח:כו–לא; הַפְטָרָה: יְחֶזְקֵאל א:א–כח וִיחֶזְקֵאל ג:יב

אַקְדָּמוּת
בְּיוֹם הָרִאשׁוֹן שֶׁל שָׁבוּעוֹת, שֶׁהַכֹּהֵן עוֹלֶה לַתּוֹרָה, וְלִפְנֵי שֶׁהוּא מְבָרֵךְ
אוֹמְרִים הַקּוֹרֵא בַּתּוֹרָה וְהַקָּהָל לְסֵירוּגִין:

Akdamut   אַקְדָּמוּת

For centuries, Jews have been conditioned by these teachings about the sanctity of life. No wonder then that the violent reaction to an attack, even in self-defense, does not come easily to the Jew. What would have been more natural for this people, singled out by the Germans for destruction, than to think of vengeance against them and to call for it. Yet even such an obvious concept as vengeance is given its specifically Jewish meaning. When Shlomo Zlichovsky died on the gallows with *Shema Yisrael* on his lips, one of the others who was hanged together with him called to the Jews who were forced to witness the murders: "Jews! Avenge our blood!" One young Jew who was present asked himself: "How and with what to take revenge? What is the purpose of vengeance? And what is real and ultimate revenge? Do we Jews have the possibility or the power to do it?" Standing facing the ten gallows on that eve of the festival of Shavuot, in spite of his youth, he understood the logical link between the two calls: "Hear, O Israel, the Eternal is

TORAH READING FOR SHAVUOT

DAY 1 TORAH READING
Read inside and outside Israel

Exodus 19:1 – 20:23; Maftir: Numbers 28:26–31; Haftarah: Ezekiel 1:1–28; Ezekiel 3:12

AKDAMUT
On the first day of Shavuot, after the Kohen is called up to
the Torah and before he makes a bracha, the following is said
responsively by the Baal Koreh and the congregation:

our God, the Eternal is One," and "Jews! Avenge our blood!" And he wrote of that day:

"This, indeed, is the greatest and surest vengeance. Above all, the Germans intended to kill the Jewish soul, to defile it. … This is the reason why they chose the eve of Shavuot, the season of the giving of the Torah by God to Israel – on that day to terrorize the Jews and to destroy their *emunah*. But Shlomo Zlichovsky proved to them in the presence of all these oppressed Jews. … that the German hangmen have no power whatever over the Jewish soul and that they are unable to uproot the trust from our hearts. This is the true vengeance; the Jewish vengeance.

"And I, too, then took revenge on the enemy. The next day, after the hangings, I joined a secret *minyan* that assembled in our house for the festival service. We received the holy Torah with joy and fervor and sang the *Akdamut* to the tune of Shlomo Zlichovsky that was vibrating within us. As if nothing had happened."

With God in Hell, pages 152–153

73

אַקְדָמוּת מִלִּין וְשָׁרָיוּת שׁוּתָא

אוּלָא שָׁקֵלְנָא הַרְמָן וּרְשׁוּתָא

בְּבָבֵי תְרֵי וּתְלַת דְאֶפְתַּח בְּנַקְשׁוּתָא

בְּבָרֵי דְבָרֵי וְטָרֵי עֲדֵי לְקַשִׁישׁוּתָא

גְבוּרָן עָלְמִין לֵהּ וְלָא סְפֵק פְּרִישׁוּתָא

גְוִיל אִלּוּ רְקִיעֵי קְנֵי כָּל חוּרְשָׁתָא

דְיוֹ אִלּוּ יַמֵּי וְכָל מֵי כְנִישׁוּתָא

דָיְרֵי אַרְעָא סָפְרֵי וְרָשְׁמֵי רַשְׁוָתָא

הֲדַר מָרֵי שְׁמַיָּא וְשַׁלִּיט בְּיַבֶּשְׁתָא

הֲקֵים עָלְמָא יְחִידָאי וְכַבְּשֵׁהּ בְּכַבְּשׁוּתָא

וּבְלָא לֵאוּ שַׁכְלְלֵהּ וּבְלָא תְשָׁשׁוּתָא

Ten Commandments
וְשָׁרָיוּת שׁוּתָא

The sacred is life's sanctification on earth. History is man's responsibility; it is one of the dimensions of sanctification. Here, within the God-given task of sanctification, is the source of man's freedom as well as of his responsibility. The God who calls man to responsibility is the guarantor of his freedom to act responsibly. As man accepts responsibility, he enters upon his God-given heritage of freedom. Or as the rabbis read it: "Freedom – on the Tablets." Granting him freedom and calling him to responsibility, God has expressed his confidence in his creature, man. This, notwithstanding man's disappointing performance in history, remains for the Jew the foundation of his optimism.

Faith After the Holocaust, page 60

בְּבָרֵי דְבָרֵי וְטָרֵי עֲדֵי לְקַשִׁישׁוּתָא
Of God who creates and ever sustains.

If the creator, having done his job, has left the world to its own devices, letting it function by way of universal laws implanted within it, then of course he is unapproachable by man as he himself does not approach man. Prayer is meaningful only on the basis of a theistic worldview. One may pray only because one is able to believe that even after the act

Before reciting the **Ten Commandments**,

I first ask permission and approval

To start with two or three stanzas in fear

Of God who creates and ever sustains.

He has endless might, not to be described

Were the skies parchment, were all the reeds quills,

Were the seas and all waters made of ink,

Were all the world's inhabitants made scribes.

The glorious Lord of heaven and earth,

Alone, formed the world, veiled in mystery.

Without exertion did he perfect it,

---

of creation, God has remained with the world, that indeed He renews daily the works of creation. One is able to believe this only within the context of revelational religion. We know of His presence because He has made His presence known; we know that He is near because He has indeed been near. We may turn to Him in prayer because He has turned to man in revelation.

Prayer, page 73

גְּבוּרָן עָלְמִין לֵהּ וְלָא סְפֵק פְּרִישׁוּתָא

He has endless might, not to be described

The question as to God's presence in history is raised on the assumption that the fear of God ought to subdue the enemies of God and the power of God ought to protect God's people. The answer is based on a radical redefinition of the concepts of the fear and the might of God. The mightiness of God is shown in his tolerance of the mocking of his enemies; it is revealed in his long suffering. This is in keeping with the interpretation of the words of the psalmist: "Who is like unto you among the mighty (Psalms 89:8 and see Exodus 15:11)," enduring insults and remaining silent. The awesomeness of God is revealed in the survival of Israel.

Faith After the Holocaust, pages 111–112

וּבְאָתָא קַלִּילָא דְּלֵית בֵּיהּ מְשֵׁשׁוּתָא
זְמִין כָּל עִיבִידְתֵּהּ בְּהַךְ יוֹמֵי שִׁתָּא
זְהוֹר יְקָרֵהּ עֲלֵי עֲלֵי כָּרְסְיֵהּ דְּאֶשָׁתָא
חֵיִל אֶלֶף אַלְפִּין וְרִבּוֹא לְשַׁמְּשׁוּתָא
חַדְתִּין נְבוֹט לְצַפְרִין סַגִּיאָה טְרָשׁוּתָא
טְפֵי יְקִידִין שְׂרָפִין כְּלוֹל גַּפֵּי שִׁתָּא
טְעֵם עַד יִתְיְהֵב לְהוֹן שְׁתִיקִין בְּאָדִישָׁתָא
יְקַבְּלוּן דֵּין מִדֵּין שָׁוֵי דְּלָא בְּשַׁשָׁתָא
יְקַר מְלֵי כָל אַרְעָא לְתַלְוֹתֵי קְדוּשָׁתָא
כְּקָל מִן קֳדָם שַׁדַּי כְּקָל מֵי נְפִישׁוּתָא
כְּרוּבִין קֳבֵל גַּלְגְּלִין מְרוֹמְמִין בְּאוֹשָׁתָא
לְמֶחֱזָא בְּאַנְפָּא עֵין כְּוָת גִּירֵי קַשְׁתָּא

---

great faith	סַגִּיאָה טְרָשׁוּתָא

In these last weeks of uneasiness, I had often to think of the great change that had taken place in the nature of the Jew. We Jews used to be accustomed to catastrophes, to Jewish and world tragedies. We have seen much, but we seem to have changed much. In former times, in the midst of tragedies, Jews were firm, quiet, and steadfast. Today we are nervous, fidgety, and doubting. Our ancestors lived by their faith and were the great masters of moral strategy. We, however, are a generation without real faith. For our ancestors, faith meant the idea of a great pattern of universal and cosmic life, devised by God and carrying a deep, though often hidden, sense. All the happenings around them, all the events of their individual lives or those appertaining to the life of the nation and of mankind, wars, epidemics, and natural catastrophes, had their appropriate place in one great Divine scheme. The scheme, as they understood it, may often seem to us naive and simple. Its greatness consisted in the fact that no event was taken at its face value, but was seen in a certain relation to the whole. A disaster did not count as such, it counted only as the part it had to play in the whole system of a life based upon faith.

We, however, are a generation without faith. Because of this, we hang

Only by a light sign, without substance.

He accomplished all his work in six days;

His glory ascended a throne of fire.

Millions of legions are at his service;

Fresh each morning they flourish with **great faith.**

More glowing are the six-winged seraphim,

Who keep silence till leave is given them.

Without delay they call to one another:

"God's majestic splendor fills the whole earth!"

Like a mighty thunder, like ocean's roar,

The cherubim and the spheres rise loudly

To gaze at the rainbowlike appearance.

---

on the words of the wireless commentator or the military spokesman; because of this we are sometimes filled with doubt and see no end to this age of darkness.

The reconstruction of life by faith is among the foremost tasks of our generation. Real faith in God will mean faith in reason and humanity. Faith in God teaches with an iron logic that wrongdoing does not pay in the long run, that it is not the way of life but of destruction and death. Once there is faith in us and the nations, the downfall of the forces of evil will be in sight.

Let us build faith in the world. Let us learn the logic of faith and the strategy of faith, and the world will appear in an entirely new light; even disasters and catastrophes will point to a happier future and a new era of hope for all men and all nations.

Between Yesterday and Tomorrow, pages 33–34

Like a mighty thunder   כְּקָל מִן קֳדָם שַׁדַּי

The Torah was given to the people of Israel. It obligates the Jew to study it and to seek to understand it; it demands of the sages of Israel that they interpret it and teach it as guidance and law for everyday living. Since the Torah was given not to angels but to human beings, and

לְכָל אֲתַר דְּמִשְׁתַּלְּחִין זְרִיזִין בְּאַשְׁוָתָא
מְבָרְכִין בְּרִיךְ יְקָרֵהּ בְּכָל לְשַׁן לְחִישׁוּתָא
מֵאֲתַר בֵּית שְׁכִינְתֵּהּ דְּלָא צְרִיךְ בְּחִישׁוּתָא
נְהֶם כָּל חֵיל מְרוֹמָא מְקַלְּסִין בַּחֲשַׁשְׁתָּא
נְהִירָא מַלְכוּתֵהּ לְדָר וְדָר לְאַפְרַשְׁתָּא
סְדִירָא בְּהוֹן קְדוּשְׁתֵּיהּ וְכַד חָלְפָא שַׁעְתָּא
סִיּוּמָא דְּלְעָלַם וְאוֹף לָא לִשְׁבוּעֲתָא
עֲדַב יְקָר אַחְסַנְתֵּהּ חֲבִיבִין דְּבִקְבַעְתָּא
עֲבִידָא לֵהּ חֲטִיבָא בְּדַנַח וּשְׁקַעְתָּא
פְּרִישָׁן לִמְנָתֵהּ לְמֶעְבַּד לֵהּ רְעוּתָא
פְּרִישְׁתֵי שְׁבָחֵהּ יְחַוּוֹן בִּשְׁעוּתָא
צְבִי וְחָמֵד וְרָגֵג דְּלָאוֹן בְּלְעוּתָא
צְלוֹתְהוֹן בְּכֵן מְקַבֵּל וְהַנְיָא בְּעוּתָא
קְטִירָא לְחַי עָלְמָא בְּתָגָא בִּשְׁבוּעֲתָא

---

since it depends on interpretation and understanding by human beings, whatever is discovered in it by human beings who accept the Torah as God's revelation to the Jewish people at Sinai and study it, is indeed the truth of the Torah. That is how the sages of Israel understood what happened at the time of God's revelation at Sinai. The psalmist says of the event that the voice of God sounded "with might." The psalmist does not say, "With his might." No human being could have survived it. The people received the voice; young and old, men, women, and children, each according to his own strength (Psalms 29:4; Exodus Rabbah 5:9; also Song of Songs Rabbah 6:3). Human beings receive even the revelation of God only with their human capacities. Once a Jew accepts the Torah from Sinai, whatever it teaches him in his search for its meaning and message is the word of God for him. The giver of the Torah to mere man accepts responsibility for it; it is Torah. Of the great discussions and sharp disagreements between the schools Shamai and Hillel, a voice from heaven was heard to proclaim: "These as well as those are words of the living God" (Eruvin 13b). The subjective human

Wherever set, they hasten anxiously,

Whispering praise in each tongue: "Blessed be

His glory in his entire universe."

All the heavenly hosts shout praise in awe:

"His glory shines forever and ever!"

Their hymn is timed; when the hour is gone,

They shall at no period chant it again.

Dear to him are the people of Israel,

Acclaiming him each morning and evening.

They are dedicated to do his will;

His wonders, his praises, they declare hourly.

He desires them to toil in the Torah,

So that their prayer be well accepted,

Bound up in the crown of the Eternal,

---

element is not to be eliminated from the acceptance of the Torah. It was included in the meaning of the Torah from the very beginning. Needless to say, there have to be principles by which to determine the halacha, the law for the people to live by.

Not in Heaven, page 77

צְבִי וְחָמַד וְרָגֵג דְּלָאוּן בְּלֵעוּתָא

He desires them to toil in the Torah

We have seen how interrelated pragmatic and moral considerations are in the halacha. We will address the power of ethics in the halacha. In his Kuzari, Judah Halevi writes: "God forbid that anything in the Torah should contradict reason." The rabbis in the Talmud were guided by the insight: God forbid that any application of the Torah to life should contradict the principles of ethics. What are those principles? They are Torah principles, such as: "And you shall do that which is right and good in the sight of the Eternal" (Deuteronomy 6:18); "Its ways are ways of pleasantness, and all its paths are peace" (according to

קַבֵּל יְקָר טוֹטַפְתָּא יְתִיבָא בְּקִבִיעָתָא

רְשִׁימָא הִיא גוּפָא בְּחָכְמְתָא וּבְדַעְתָּא

רְבוּתָא דְּיִשְׂרָאֵל קְרָאֵי בִּשְׁמַעְתָּא

שְׁבַח רִבּוֹן עָלְמָא אֲמִירָא דִּכְוָתָא

שְׁפַר עֲלֵי לְחַוּיֵהּ בְּאַפֵּי מַלְכְּוָתָא

תְּאֵין וּמִתְכַּנְּשִׁין כְּחֶזּוּ אִדְוָתָא

תְּמֵהִין וְשָׁיְלִין לֵהּ בְּעֵסֶק אַתְוָתָא

מְנָן וּמָאן הוּא רְחִימָךְ שַׁפְּרָא בְּרֵוָתָא

אֲרוּם בְּגִינֵהּ סָפֵית מְדוֹר אַרְיָוָתָא

יַקְרָא וְיָאָה אַתְּ אִין תֵּעְרְבִי לְמַרְוָתָא

רְעוּתִיךְ נַעֲבֵד לִיךְ בְּכָל אַתְרָוָתָא

בְּחָכְמְתָא מְתִיבָא לְהוֹן קְצָת לְהוֹדָעוּתָא

יְדַעְתּוּן חַכְמִין לֵהּ בְּאִשְׁתְּמוֹדָעוּתָא

רְבוּתְכוֹן מֶה חֲשִׁיבָא קַבֵּל הַהִיא שְׁבַחְתָּא

רְבוּתָא דְּיַעֲבֵד לִי כִּי כִי מָטְיָא יְשׁוּעָתָא

---

talmudic teaching, this refers to the ways and the paths of the Torah) (Proverbs 3:17); or "That you may walk in the way of good people, and guard the paths of the righteous" (Proverbs 2:20). In summation of such principles, the Talmud would say: "The Torah in its entirety exists for the sake of the ways of peace" (Gitin 59b). Quite clearly, these principles, and such an understanding of the meaning of the Torah, give priority to the ethical demand. This priority influences biblical interpretation. It reaches out beyond strict legality, and it even renders explicit biblical commandments inapplicable.

Not in Heaven, pages 28–29

יַקְרָא וְיָאָה אַתְּ אִין תֵּעְרְבִי לְמַרְוָתָא
Most precious are you; if you merge with us

There is a natural affinity between mysticism and pantheism. All mysticism tends toward pantheism. Once the mystical union is completed there is nothing left but the Absolute, in which all is contained. The

Securely set near the precious frontlet.

His frontlet is most skillfully inscribed:

"Great is Israel who proclaims God's Oneness."

The praise of the world's Lord, in pure homage,

I am pleased to declare before the kings.

They come and gather like the surging waves,

Wondering and asking about the signs:

Whence and who is your beloved, O fair one?

For whom do you die in the lion's den?

Most precious are you; if you merge with us,

We will do your will in all the regions.

With wisdom I answer them concisely:

You must recognize and acknowledge him!

Of what value is your glory compared

With all that God will do for me in due time,

---

appropriate worldview of the mystic is pantheism. It is his justification for devaluing individual existence, as well as for attempting to redeem it through a return into the All. On the other hand, mysticism is the only available "religion" for the pantheist. His worship of the Absolute demands the denial of his own personal separateness from it. Thus, we are led to the Spinozistic *amor dei*: since nothing exists apart from the infinite, man's love for God "is the very love of God with which God loves Himself." One is inclined to agree with those who see in this the monstrous example of absolute self-love. The truth, of course, is that where there is no separateness, there is no love either. Where there is no encounter, there can be no care or concern. The mystic endeavors to overcome all separateness, while the pantheist denies it from the very beginning. Judaism, on the other hand, through its concept of the encounter, affirms the reality as well as the worth of separate and individual existence. Judaism is not only non-mystical; it is also essentially anti-pantheistic.

God, Man and History, page 40

בְּמֵיתֵי לִי נְהוֹרָא וְתִחֲפֵי לְכוֹן בַּהֲתָא

יְקָרֵהּ כַּד אִתְגְּלִי בְּתָקְפָּא וּבִגְוָיָתָא

יְשַׁלֵּם גְּמַלְיָא לְשָׂנְאֵי וְנַגְוָתָא

צִדְקָתָא לְעַם חַבִּיב וְסַגִּי זַכְוָתָא

חֲדוּ שְׁלָמָא בְּמֵיתֵי וּמָנָא דַכְוָתָא

קִרְיָתָא דִירוּשְׁלֵם כַּד יְכַנֵּשׁ גַּלְוָתָא

יְקָרֵהּ כַּד אִתְגְּלִי בְּתָקְפָּא וּבִגְוָיָתָא

When He will reveal himself in great might

Bolder still than the prophets were the teachers of the Talmud, who possessed sufficient spiritual courage to make the daring statement: "Where you find the mightiness of the Holy One, blessed be He, there you find also His humility" (Megilla 31a). The humility of God is a frightening term; yet, God's concern for lowly man cannot be explained in any other way. In the encounter, it is God's self-denial that 'sets man upon his feet." One might, perhaps, say that only through divine humility is man granted the strength of individuality to be able to endure, be it even for one single glimpse, the slightest inkling of divine mightiness. In the very terror of the encounter, man is being affirmed.

God, Man and History, page 37

He will repay the foes in all the isles   יְשַׁלֵּם גְּמַלְיָא לְשָׂנְאֵי וְנַגְוָתָא

Yet all this does not exonerate God for all the suffering of the innocent in history. God is responsible for having created a world in which man is free to make history. There must be a dimension beyond history in which all suffering finds its redemption through God. This is essential to the faith of a Jew. The Jew does not doubt God's presence, though he is unable to set limits to the duration and intensity of his absence. This is no justification for the ways of providence, but its acceptance. It is not a willingness to forgive the unheard cries of millions, but a trust that in God the tragedy of man may find its transformation. Within time and history that cry is unforgivable. One of the teachers of the Talmud notes that when God asks Abraham to offer him his son Isaac as a sacrifice, the exact rendering of the biblical words reads: "Take, I pray

When light will come to me and shame to you,

When He will reveal himself in great might?

He will repay the foes in all the isles;

Triumph to the dear and upright people!

Perfect joy, pure delight, will come into

Jerusalem **when He will gather the exiles.**

---

thee, thy son." In the view of this teacher the "binding of Isaac" was not a command of God, but a request that Abraham take upon himself this most exacting of all God's impositions (Sanhedrin 89b). In a sense, we see in this a recognition that the sacrificial way of the innocent through history is not to be vindicated or justified! It remains unforgivable. God himself has to ask an Abraham to favor him by accepting the imposition of such a sacrifice. The divine request accompanies all those through history who suffer for the only reason that God created man, whom God himself has to endure. Within time and history God remains indebted to his people; he may be long-suffering only at their expense. It was hardly ever as true as in our own days, after the holocaust. Is it perhaps what God desires – a people, to whom He owes so much, who yet acknowledge Him? Children, who have every reason to condemn His creation, yet accept the creator in the faith that in the fullness of time, the divine indebtedness will be redeemed and the divine adventure with man will be approved even by its martyred victims?

Faith After the Holocaust, pages 139–140

when He will gather the exiles   כַּד יְכַנֵּשׁ גַּלְוָתָא

There are many passages in the Talmud and Midrash that describe God as weeping over the exile of His children (Brachot 59a). This is in keeping with our earlier analysis that God, having created man, rendered Himself "powerless" in a sense. Why should exile involve the kind of suffering Israel had to endure? It is taken for granted that a minority scattered all over the world that attempts to retain its identity will be oppressed and persecuted. But this can only be taken for granted because there is something very wrong with man and with the world.

יְקָרָה מַטִּיל עֲלַהּ בְּיוֹמֵי וְלֵילְוָתָא

גְּנוּנֵהּ לְמֶעְבַּד בַּהּ בְּתוּשְׁבְּחָן כְּלִילָתָא

דְּזֵהוֹר עֲנָנַיָּא לְמִשְׁפַּר כִּילָתָא

לְפוּמָא דַּעֲבִידְתָּא עֲבִידָן מְטַלָתָא

בְּתַכְתִּקֵי דְּהַב פִּזָּא וְשֶׁבַע מְעָלָתָא

תְּחִימִין צַדִּיקֵי קֳדָם רַב פָּעֳלָתָא

וּרְוֵיהוֹן דָּמֵי לְשַׁבְעָא חֶדְוָתָא

רְקִיעָא בְּזֵהוֹרֵהּ וְכוֹכְבֵי זִיוָתָא

הֲדָרָא דְּלָא אֶפְשַׁר לְמִפְרַט סְפוָתָא

וְלָא אִשְׁתְּמַע וַחֲמֵי נְבִיאָן חֶזְוָתָא

בְּלָא שָׁלְטָא בֵּהּ עַיִן בְּגוֹ עֵדֶן גִּנְתָא

מְטַיְּלֵי בֵּי חִנְגָּא לְבַהֲדֵי דִשְׁכִינְתָּא

עֲלַהּ רָמְזֵי דֵין הוּא בְּרַם בְּאֶמְתָנוּתָא

שְׁבַּרְנָא לֵהּ בְּשִׁבְיָן תְּקוֹף הֵימָנוּתָא

Whenever a minority is persecuted, justice, humanity, and decency are all in a state of exile from the affairs of men. The case of the Jew is, of course, aggravated by the fact that, not by what he does, but by what he is, indeed by the fact that he is, represents a challenge to the principle by which nations "normally" live. And God himself is "powerless." He could crush man and destroy man's world. But if He desires man, He must take the risk with Him and wait for him until man becomes what he ought to be. This, of course, means that exile is a cosmic condition. God himself is a refugee in the world. This is the final meaning of the Jewish concept of *shekhinta beGaluta*, the Divine Presence in exile in the world. The *galut* of the Jewish people is a specific case of this cosmic condition and a necessary outcome of it.

Faith After the Holocaust, pages 126–127

His glory will shield Zion day and night,

While his tent for praise will be made in it

Under a splendid canopy of bright clouds.

For each godly man a booth will be made,

Furnished with a gold throne of seven steps.

The righteous will be arrayed before God,

Their sights resembling sevenfold delight,

The brilliant sky and the luminous stars –

A splendor that no language can describe,

That was not heard of nor viewed by prophets.

No eye has penetrated Paradise,

Where the righteous dance in presence of God,

Reverently pointing out: "This is He

For whom we looked in exile with firm faith!

שְׂבַרְנָא לֵהּ בְּשִׁבְיָן תְּקוֹף הֵימָנוּתָא

For whom we looked in exile with firm faith

It would seem then that, overall, we have to go our own way. We have to work hard to make Judaism a significant philosophy of life in the intellectual climate of our age. We have to prove it to be a significant form of living that takes due cognizance of the moral predicaments of our days. We must equip it with the ability to articulate the truth of God in relationship to the vital issues of present-day human existence. If, as we develop our own position in the intellectual, ethical, theological, and religious realms of twentieth-century human endeavor, we find other religions working beside us, all the better. If not, we shall not be concerned. An awe-inspiring task lies ahead of us. Hard work, challenging and exacting, is to be done on the interpretation of Judaism and its implementation in this new era. We have every reason to continue with faith and confidence in our path. This is one of those rare turning points in history when we feel the breath of eternity about us. Having survived miraculously, the world-historic mystery of Israel has been deepened

יַדְבֵּר לָן עָלְמִין עָלְמִין מְדַמּוּתָא

מְנָת דְּלָן דְּמִלְּקַדְמִין פָּרֵשׁ בְּאָרְמוּתָא

טְלִילָא דִּלְוְיָתָן וְתוֹר טוּר רָמוּתָא

וְחַד בְּחַד כִּי סָבִיךְ וְעָבֵד קְרָבוּתָא

בְּקַרְנוֹהִי מְנַגַּח בְּהֵמוֹת בִּרְבוּתָא

יְקַרְטַע נוּן לְקָבְלֵהּ בְּצִיצוֹי בִּגְבוּרְתָּא

מְקָרֵב לֵהּ בָּרְיֵהּ בְּחַרְבֵּהּ בְּרַבְרְבוּתָא

אֲרִסְטוֹן לְצַדִּיקֵי יְתַקֵּן וְשֵׁרוּתָא

מְסַחֲרִין עֲלֵי תַּכֵּי דְכַדְכוֹד וְגוּמַרְתָּא

נְגִידִין קָמֵיהוֹן אֲפַרְסְמוֹן נַהֲרָתָא

וּמִתְפַּנְקֵי וְרָווֹ בְּכַסֵּי רְוָיָתָא

חֲמַר מְרַת דְּמִבְּרֵאשִׁית נְטִיר בֵּי נַעֲוָתָא

זַכָּאִין כִּי שְׁמַעְתּוּן שְׁבַח דָּא שִׁירָתָא

קְבִיעִין כֵּן תֶּהֱווֹן בְּהַנְהוּ חֲבוּרְתָּא

וְתִזְכּוּן דִּי תֵיתְבוּן בְּעֵלָּא דָרְתָא

אֲרֵי תְצִיתוּן לְמִלּוֹי דְנָפְקִין בְּהַדְרָתָא

מְרוֹמָם הוּא אֱלָהִין בְּקַדְמְתָא וּבַתְרַיְתָא

צְבִי וְאִתְרְעִי בָן וּמְסַר לָן אוֹרַיְתָא

---

ever more by Israel's return to the land of its origins in accordance with the faith of the dark centuries of homelessness.

Faith After the Holocaust, page 47

He now gently guides us eternally   יַדְבֵּר לָן עָלְמִין עָלְמִין מְדַמּוּתָא

The Rabbis in the Talmud saw the mightiness of the Almighty in that He controls His inclination to judge and to punish and behaves in history as if He were powerless. To curb the use of power where infinite power is at hand, to endure the mocking of one's enemies when one could easily eliminate them, that is true strength. Such is the might-iness of God. God is mighty, for He shackles His omnipotence and

He now gently guides us eternally,

Granting us the share long reserved for us.

Leviathan contends with Behemoth;

They are locked in combat with each other.

Behemoth gores mightily with its horns;

The sea-monster counters with potent fins.

The Creator slays them with his great sword,

And prepares a banquet for the righteous,

Who sit in rows at tables of precious stones,

While before them there flow streams of balsam,

And they indulge themselves and drink full cups

Of the precious old wine preserved in vats.

You upright, having heard this hymn of praise,

May you be in that blissful company!

You will merit to sit in the first row

If you will obey God's majestic words.

God, exalted from beginning to end,

Was pleased with us and gave us the Torah.

---

becomes "powerless" so that history may be possible. In spite of His infinite power, He does not frighten man but lets him find his own way, extending to him His longsuffering. God is mighty in the renunciation of His might in order to bear with man. Yet He is present in history. He reveals his presence in the survival of his people Israel. Therein lies His awesomeness. God renders Himself powerless, as it were, through forbearance and long-suffering, yet He guides. How else could His powerless people have survived! He protects, without manifest power. Because of that, Israel could endure God's long silences without denying Him.

Faith After the Holocaust, page 112

רִאשׁוֹן

בַּחֹ֙דֶשׁ֙ הַשְּׁלִישִׁ֔י לְצֵ֥את בְּנֵֽי־יִשְׂרָאֵ֖ל מֵאֶ֣רֶץ מִצְרָ֑יִם בַּיּ֣וֹם הַזֶּ֔ה בָּ֖אוּ מִדְבַּ֥ר סִינָֽי׃ ²וַיִּסְע֣וּ מֵרְפִידִ֗ים וַיָּבֹ֙אוּ֙ מִדְבַּ֣ר סִינַ֔י וַֽיַּחֲנ֖וּ בַּמִּדְבָּ֑ר וַיִּֽחַן־שָׁ֥ם יִשְׂרָאֵ֖ל נֶ֥גֶד הָהָֽר׃ ³וּמֹשֶׁ֥ה עָלָ֖ה אֶל־הָֽאֱלֹהִ֑ים וַיִּקְרָ֙א אֵלָ֤יו יְהֹוָה֙ מִן־הָהָ֣ר לֵאמֹ֔ר כֹּ֤ה תֹאמַר֙ לְבֵ֣ית יַעֲקֹ֔ב וְתַגֵּ֖יד לִבְנֵ֥י יִשְׂרָאֵֽל׃ ⁴אַתֶּ֣ם רְאִיתֶ֔ם אֲשֶׁ֥ר עָשִׂ֖יתִי לְמִצְרָ֑יִם וָאֶשָּׂ֤א אֶתְכֶם֙ עַל־כַּנְפֵ֣י נְשָׁרִ֔ים וָאָבִ֥א אֶתְכֶ֖ם אֵלָֽי׃ ⁵וְעַתָּ֗ה אִם־שָׁמ֤וֹעַ תִּשְׁמְעוּ֙ בְּקֹלִ֔י וּשְׁמַרְתֶּ֖ם אֶת־בְּרִיתִ֑י וִהְיִ֙יתֶם לִ֤י סְגֻלָּה֙ מִכׇּל־הָ֣עַמִּ֔ים כִּֽי־

כֹּ֤ה תֹאמַר֙ לְבֵ֣ית יַעֲקֹ֔ב וְתַגֵּ֖יד לִבְנֵ֥י יִשְׂרָאֵֽל

So shall you say to the house of Jacob and tell the children of Israel

No wonder that such evaluation of women's character has led to their social exclusion in a twofold sense: neither their intelligence nor their character was trusted. According to the Midrash, a woman's lack of intelligence is even asserted in the Torah. This is derived from the passage in Exodus where Moses is told how to communicate the teaching to the Jewish people. The text reads: "Thus shall you speak to the house of Jacob and tell the children of Israel" (Exodus 28:2). Undoubtedly there is a difference in meaning and emphasis between the Hebrew *tomar*, "to say, speak," and *taggid*, which connotes a more comprehensive and intense communication. At the same time, the phrase "the house of Jacob" is usually interpreted as referring to the women. The result is the following interpretation: "'Thus shall you speak to the house of Jacob' – these are the women. Give them *roshei devarim*, a short summary of the themes that they will be able to understand; 'and tell the children of Israel' – these are the men. They are to be taught the subjects minutest detail, for they are able to understand them" (Midrash Rabba). It is taken for granted that the intelligence of women is quite inferior to

First Aliyah

In the third month of the children of Israel's departure from Egypt, on this day they arrived in the desert of Sinai. ²They journeyed from Rephidim, and they arrived in the desert of Sinai, and they encamped in the desert, and Israel encamped there opposite the mountain. ³Moses ascended to God, and the Lord called to him from the mountain, saying, "**So shall you speak to the house of Jacob and tell the children of Israel**, ⁴You have seen what I did to the Egyptians, and [how] I bore you on eagles' wings, and I brought you to Me. ⁵And now, if you obey Me and keep My covenant, **you shall be to Me a treasure out of all peoples**, for Mine is the entire earth. ⁶And

---

that of men; they are unable to study and to understand Torah. Such an evaluation of female intelligence has, of course certain halachic consequences.

Jewish Women in Time and Torah, pages 19–20

וִהְיִיתֶם לִי סְגֻלָּה מִכָּל־הָעַמִּים

you shall be to Me a treasure out of all peoples

God needs a small and relatively weak people in order to introduce another dimension into history – human life – not by might nor by power but by His spirit (See Zecharia 4:6). "The Eternal did not love you nor choose you because you were more numerous than any other people" (Deuteronomy 7:7); He could not associate His cause with the mighty and the numerous. It is not through them that a God who renders Himself "powerless" in history, for the sake of man, can advance His purpose for man. Only a nation whose presence in and impact on history testify to God's presence may be God's people. God's relation to human history is such that He needs a chosen people. The chosen people satisfy a need for divine concern for all men. Why the Jews? No matter whom He would have chosen, they would have to become Jews.

Faith After the Holocaust, page 118

לִי כָּל־הָאָרֶץ: ⁶וְאַתֶּם תִּהְיוּ־לִי מַמְלֶכֶת כֹּהֲנִים וְגוֹי קָדוֹשׁ אֵלֶּה הַדְּבָרִים
אֲשֶׁר תְּדַבֵּר אֶל־בְּנֵי יִשְׂרָאֵל:

שני

⁷וַיָּבֹא מֹשֶׁה וַיִּקְרָא לְזִקְנֵי הָעָם וַיָּשֶׂם לִפְנֵיהֶם אֵת כָּל־הַדְּבָרִים הָאֵלֶּה
אֲשֶׁר צִוָּהוּ יְהֹוָה: ⁸וַיַּעֲנוּ כָל־הָעָם יַחְדָּו וַיֹּאמְרוּ כֹּל אֲשֶׁר־דִּבֶּר יְהֹוָה
נַעֲשֶׂה וַיָּשֶׁב מֹשֶׁה אֶת־דִּבְרֵי הָעָם אֶל־יְהֹוָה: ⁹וַיֹּאמֶר יְהֹוָה אֶל־מֹשֶׁה

---

a kingdom of priests and a holy nation   מַמְלֶכֶת כֹּהֲנִים וְגוֹי קָדוֹשׁ

The historic mission of Israel has therefore been described by the Bible
in the declaration: "And you shall be unto me a kingdom of priests, and
a holy nation" (Exodus 19:6). This kingdom of priests is not a society in
which a priestly caste rules over an unpriestly populace in the name of
some god. A holy nation is a realm in which all are priests. But where
all are priests, all are servants – and God alone rules. A "kingdom of
priests and a holy nation" is thus not a theocracy, but a God-centered
republic.

God, Man and History, pages 140–141

---

we shall do   נַעֲשֶׂה

A survivor of Buchenwald was walking back to the camp, soon after
its liberation, having helped bury the mounds of bodies that had been
dumped all over the camp. He was pondering the words of the *Kaddish*
that he would recite over the mass graves: "Magnified and exalted be
His great name." What would now become of the Jewish people, what
of Judaism, after this incomprehensible disaster? To him, the face of
every Jewish inmate in the camp mirrored a vivid picture of the Jewish
people. A crippled and shrunken people, a race which had suffered the
most tremendous spiritual, as well as physical, onslaught in the history
of mankind; a race of orphans, widows, and widowers; a race of mourn-
ing fathers, of saddened mothers whose babies had been snatched away
from their breasts; of sons who have seen their fathers, brothers, and
sisters burnt to ashes while still half-alive. He was wondering if anyone
would care to hear again of God, Judaism, or religion. Yes, of course,

you shall be to Me **a kingdom of priests and a holy nation**.' These are the words that you shall speak to the children of Israel."

Second Aliyah

[7] Moses came and summoned the elders of Israel and placed before them all these words that the Lord had commanded him. [8] And the nation replied in unison and said, "All that the Lord has spoken **we shall do!**" and Moses took the words of the people back to the Lord. [9] And the Lord said to Moses, "Behold, I am coming to you in the thickness

---

the liberators would now all come and provide the survivors with food, drugs, and medical aid. The Americans would flood them with cigarettes, chocolate, and vitamins. But who would provide the religious serum which was so necessary to instill some spirit of Godliness into a hopeless, crushed, people? His father, who could have guided him in that hour of mental anguish, was no longer. Where was he to turn? Where to go? How to start anew? To his great surprise, it was right there, in the midst of the pyres of the camp, in the hell of Buchenwald, that he found himself, and experienced what he called his religious revival. A few days before his scheduled departure from Buchenwald, an announcement came over the camp loudspeaker that the Jewish chaplain to the American forces would be conducting religious services that evening, which was the beginning of Shavuot, the festival of the Torah revelation at Sinai.

He wondered: was this not too early? Were not the survivors being put to the test too soon? Who among those thousands of physical and mental cripples would want to attend services and prayers so soon after their tragic experience? The festival of receiving the Torah! Indeed! Our survivor felt that the loudspeaker announcement was a challenge to all of them and to their loyalties. But this is how he summed up the camp's response to the challenge:

"...just as you cannot measure the physical strength of an oppressed people, so you cannot gauge its spiritual wealth and power. On that evening, Buchenwald staged a unique demonstration of faith and loyalty to God. Thousands of liberated Jews crowded into the specifically vacated block for the first postwar Jewish religious service to be held on the soil of defeated Germany. The Muselmänner, the cripples, the injured, and the weak came to demonstrate to the world that the last

הִנֵּה אָנֹכִי בָּא אֵלֶיךָ בְּעַב הֶעָנָן בַּעֲבוּר יִשְׁמַע הָעָם בְּדַבְּרִי עִמָּךְ וְגַם־בְּךָ
יַאֲמִינוּ לְעוֹלָם וַיַּגֵּד מֹשֶׁה אֶת־דִּבְרֵי הָעָם אֶל־יְהוָה: וַיֹּאמֶר יְהוָה אֶל־
מֹשֶׁה לֵךְ אֶל־הָעָם וְקִדַּשְׁתָּם הַיּוֹם וּמָחָר וְכִבְּסוּ שִׂמְלֹתָם: וְהָיוּ נְכֹנִים

---

ounce of their strength, the last drop of their blood, and the last breaths of their lives belonged to God, to Torah, and to the Jewish religion.

As Chaplain Schechter intoned the evening prayers, all the inmates in and outside the block stood in silence, reaccepting the Torah whose people, message, and purpose Hitler's Germany attempted to destroy. Jewish history repeated itself. Just as our forefathers who were liberated from Egypt accepted the law in the desert, so did we, the liberated Jews of Buchenwald, reaccept the same Law in a concentration camp in Germany."

With God in Hell, pages 23–25

and they will also believe in you forever   וְגַם־בְּךָ יַאֲמִינוּ לְעוֹלָם

In order to understand how serious is the spiritual position of Judaism, we must not forget that Judaism originally was not lacking in the potentiality of development. The prophets and their successors, the teachers of the Mishnah and Gemara, were not orthodox Jews in the sense in which we understand the word today; and to try and compare them with anything liberal would be quite devoid of meaning. The Talmud tells us, for instance, that Rabbi Eliezer, in a controversy with Rabbi Joshua, called for miracles to testify to the truth of his opinion, and in the end a voice from Heaven (*Bat-Kol*) declared that everywhere the opinion of Rabbi Eliezer was decisive halacha. And yet Rabbi Joshua was able to say, "The Torah is no more in the Heaven, we are not obliged to obey the miraculous voice from Heaven." Such a Judaism, claiming an independence that could not be influenced either by miracles or even by a direct "message from Heaven," was surely not lacking in boldness or intellectual courage. In an *Aggadah*, in the tractate Menachot (29b), the story is told that when God introduced Moses in the *Beit-Hamidrash* of Rabbi Akiva, Moses was unable to follow the lectures of that great master, and only regained his peace of mind when he heard Rabbi Akiva replying to a pupil that his (Rabbi Akiva's) teaching was nothing new but tradition directly received by Moses from Sinai. An *Aggadah* like this, expresses in a striking manner the evolutionary unfolding of

of the cloud, in order that the nation shall hear when I speak to you, **and they will also believe in you forever.**" And Moses relayed the words of the people to the Lord. [10] And the Lord said to Moses, **"Go to the people and prepare them today and tomorrow**, and

---

Judaism in the course of Jewish history. Not even Moses himself is able to recognize the Judaism of Rabbi Akiva at first glance, for it is somehow different, something new. Nevertheless, it is still *Torat Mosheh*, for it is indeed the teaching of Moses, organically unfolding itself in the life of the nation. Everywhere in Talmud and Midrash, we meet this courage to apply the spirit of the ancient word to new situations and in so doing to give the word a new shape. The Torah is not eternal in the sense that it retains for all time that shape in which it was first understood by men. It is eternal because it has the miraculous power to reveal to each generation new meanings which are yet the old ones, which have waited just for this generation to be lifted into the sun of the passing day.

Towards Historic Judaism, pages 29–30

לֵךְ אֶל־הָעָם וְקִדַּשְׁתָּם הַיּוֹם וּמָחָר
Go to the people and prepare them today and tomorrow

According to our main argument, no regeneration of Judaism is possible without the renewal of Jewish national existence in the Jewish National Home. Only in the National Home can we create the full Jewish existence that Judaism has lacked since the destruction of the Temple, and without which harmonic and normal organic development is stunted and complete realization impossible. We have further argued that the upbuilding of the new Jewish life in Eretz Israel must be guided by historic continuity; and that, as this continuity is already broken, we must restore it by giving ourselves back to the past, filling ourselves with it, through the rediscovery of Judaism. This implies that the problems inherent in our present existence, the great religious and cultural problems of modern Jewry, are, for the time being, insoluble. Judaism is in fetters at present. It is bound by its historically determined rigidity, as a result of which it is now lacking the elasticity which it originally possessed, and which is needed to give answers to the changing questions of changing generations. For a long time to come,

לַיּוֹם הַשְּׁלִישִׁי כִּי ׀ בַּיּוֹם הַשְּׁלִשִׁי יֵרֵד יְהֹוָה לְעֵינֵי כָל־הָעָם עַל־הַר סִינָי:

יב וְהִגְבַּלְתָּ אֶת־הָעָם סָבִיב לֵאמֹר הִשָּׁמְרוּ לָכֶם עֲלוֹת בָּהָר וּנְגֹעַ בְּקָצֵהוּ

כָּל־הַנֹּגֵעַ בָּהָר מוֹת יוּמָת: יג לֹא־תִגַּע בּוֹ יָד כִּי־סָקוֹל יִסָּקֵל אוֹ־יָרֹה יִיָּרֶה

אִם־בְּהֵמָה אִם־אִישׁ לֹא יִחְיֶה בִּמְשֹׁךְ הַיֹּבֵל הֵמָּה יַעֲלוּ בָהָר:

שלישי

יד וַיֵּרֶד מֹשֶׁה מִן־הָהָר אֶל־הָעָם וַיְקַדֵּשׁ אֶת־הָעָם וַיְכַבְּסוּ שִׂמְלֹתָם:

טו וַיֹּאמֶר אֶל־הָעָם הֱיוּ נְכֹנִים לִשְׁלֹשֶׁת יָמִים אַל־תִּגְּשׁוּ אֶל־אִשָּׁה: טז וַיְהִי

בַיּוֹם הַשְּׁלִישִׁי בִּהְיֹת הַבֹּקֶר וַיְהִי קֹלֹת וּבְרָקִים וְעָנָן כָּבֵד עַל־הָהָר וְקֹל

---

we shall have to exercise very great patience. We must extricate Judaism from its fetters, free it from its rigidity, and place it in a position to give a reply at some future date to the questions of the passing day from its platform of eternity. Ours is the task to prepare Judaism for the future in such a way that our children or children's children can begin to solve the problems of modern Jewry.

Towards Historic Judaism, page 76

they may ascend the mountain   הֵמָּה יַעֲלוּ בָהָר

The ritualistic rules regarding the treatment of sanctified places and objects also have their spiritual counterpart. We find it in Psalm 24.

Who shall ascend into the mountain of the Lord: And who shall stand in the place of His holiness? He that has clean hands and a pure heart. Who hath not taken My name in vain and hath not sworn deceitfully (24:3–4).

Because God is near, man may ascend to the place of His holiness. Because he may ascend, he should ascend. Since he should ascend, let him know how to ascend. Let him accept His nearness by drawing near. Let him sanctify Him, who by revealing His will and His law for man, sanctified man.

Man and God, pages 209–210

they shall wash their garments. ¹¹ And they shall be prepared for the third day, for on the third day, the Lord will descend before the eyes of all the people upon Mount Sinai. ¹² And you shall set boundaries for the people around, saying, 'Beware of ascending the mountain or touching its edge; whoever touches the mountain shall surely be put to death.' ¹³ No hand shall touch it, for he shall be stoned or cast down; whether man or beast, he shall not live. When the ram's horn sounds a long, drawn-out blast, **they may ascend the mountain**."

Third Aliyah

¹⁴ So Moses descended from the mountain to the people, and he prepared the people, and they washed their garments. ¹⁵ He said to the people, "Be ready for three days; do not go near a woman." ¹⁶ It came to pass on the third day when it was morning, that there were **thunder claps and lightning flashes**, and a thick cloud was upon

---

thunder claps and lightning flashes   וַיְהִי קֹלֹת וּבְרָקִים

In order to catch a glimpse of the nature of the biblical encounter, we must see how the confrontation is described by those who actually experienced it. When God reveals himself at Sinai, the people are overwhelmed with terror and trembling. This need not be attributed to the phenomena of the thunder and the lightning. It is the experience of the actual encounter itself that threatens to crush them. Only part of the revelation is addressed to them directly; the people cannot endure the full power of the divine word. Buber occasionally indicates that the encounter has to be endured. However, what he means by it is something quite different from the biblical significance of the idea. Buber maintains that "to endure the revelation is to endure this moment full of possible decisions, to respond and to be responsible for every moment." Undoubtedly, an entirely different kind of a test is implied in a biblical revelation whose quality is reflected, for instance, in these words of Deuteronomy: "Behold, the Lord our God hath shown us His glory and His greatness, and we have heard His voice out of the midst of the fire; we have seen this day that God doth speak with man, and he liveth. Now, therefore, why should we die? For this great fire will consume us; if we hear the voice of the Lord our God any more, we

שֹׁפָר חָזֵק מְאֹד וַיֶּחֱרַד כָּל־הָעָם אֲשֶׁר בַּמַּחֲנֶה: ¹⁷וַיּוֹצֵא מֹשֶׁה אֶת־הָעָם לִקְרַאת הָאֱלֹהִים מִן־הַמַּחֲנֶה וַיִּתְיַצְּבוּ בְּתַחְתִּית הָהָר: ¹⁸וְהַר סִינַי עָשַׁן כֻּלּוֹ מִפְּנֵי אֲשֶׁר יָרַד עָלָיו יְהוָה בָּאֵשׁ וַיַּעַל עֲשָׁנוֹ כְּעֶשֶׁן הַכִּבְשָׁן וַיֶּחֱרַד כָּל־הָהָר מְאֹד: ¹⁹וַיְהִי קוֹל הַשֹּׁפָר הוֹלֵךְ וְחָזֵק מְאֹד מֹשֶׁה יְדַבֵּר וְהָאֱלֹהִים יַעֲנֶנּוּ בְקוֹל:

---

shall die...." There is no reciprocity here, no mutuality. On the contrary, the Thou is so overwhelming that it threatens to extinguish the reality of the I completely. All other biblical testimonies as to the nature of the experience are of a similar kind. About his encounters with the Divine, Ezekiel reports: "I fell upon my face, and I heard a voice of one that spoke" (Deuteronomy 5:21–22). The context shows that this falling upon the face is due to human weakness. The force of the vision saps the strength of the prophet. He cannot stand up and confront the Divine. Most impressively is the nature of the experience described by Daniel when he says: "So I was left alone and saw this great vision, and there remained no strength in me; for my comeliness was turned in me into corruption, and I retained no strength. Yet I heard the voice of his words; and when I heard the voice of his words, then I was fallen into a deep sleep on my face, with my face toward the ground" (Ezekiel 1:28). Far from entering a relation of mutuality in the encounter with the Divine, man becomes aware of his utter helplessness in the presence of God.

It is true, the I is nevertheless not extinguished. It is sustained, but by the mercy of God alone.

Major Themes in Modern Philosophies of Judaism, pages 106–107

the mountain, and a very powerful blast of a shofar, and the entire nation that was in the camp shuddered. [17] Moses brought the people out toward God from the camp, and they stood at the bottom of the mountain. [18] And the entire Mount Sinai smoked because the Lord had descended upon it in fire, and its smoke ascended like the smoke of the kiln, and the entire mountain quaked violently. [19] The sound of the shofar grew increasingly stronger; Moses would speak and **God would answer him with a voice.**

God would answer him with a voice　　　　וְהָאֱלֹהִים יַעֲנֶנּוּ בְקוֹל

Commenting on Psalms 29:4, "The voice of God [came] with power," Rashi says: "At the time of the giving of the Torah, God limited His voice in accordance with the strength of the Israelites to receive." The thought is developed with greater clarity in the Midrash on Exodus. It is noted that the psalmist does not say that the voice of God was heard "with His power" but simply "with power." The meaning is that standing at Sinai, each one received the Voice in accordance with his own strength: the old people in accordance with their strength, and so also the young ones, the children, and the women – each group heard it commensurate with its own strength. It is true that the reference here is to physical capacity. Had God spoken to them with the might of His strength, no one could have endured it. Each received the Voice at a pitch appropriate to his or her hearing capacity. But if this was true of the physical quality of the Voice, how much more is it evident that they all received the same word, but each in conformity with his own spiritual and moral capacity. There is no other way of receiving the meaning of any communication.

Jewish Women in Time and Torah, page 45

רביעי

כּוַיֵּ֨רֶד יְהוָֹה֙ עַל־הַ֣ר סִינַ֔י אֶל־רֹ֖אשׁ הָהָ֑ר וַיִּקְרָ֨א יְהוָֹ֧ה לְמֹשֶׁ֛ה אֶל־רֹ֥אשׁ הָהָ֖ר וַיַּ֥עַל מֹשֶֽׁה: כאוַיֹּ֤אמֶר יְהוָֹה֙ אֶל־מֹשֶׁ֔ה רֵ֖ד הָעֵ֣ד בָּעָ֑ם פֶּן־יֶהֶרְס֤וּ אֶל־יְהוָֹה֙ לִרְא֔וֹת וְנָפַ֥ל מִמֶּ֖נּוּ רָֽב: כבוְגַ֧ם הַכֹּהֲנִ֛ים הַנִּגָּשִׁ֥ים אֶל־יְהוָֹ֖ה יִתְקַדָּ֑שׁוּ פֶּן־יִפְרֹ֥ץ בָּהֶ֖ם יְהוָֹֽה: כגוַיֹּ֤אמֶר מֹשֶׁה֙ אֶל־יְהוָֹ֔ה לֹא־יוּכַ֣ל הָעָ֔ם לַעֲלֹ֖ת אֶל־הַ֣ר סִינָ֑י כִּֽי־אַתָּ֞ה הַעֵדֹ֤תָה בָּ֙נוּ֙ לֵאמֹ֔ר הַגְבֵּ֥ל אֶת־הָהָ֖ר וְקִדַּשְׁתּֽוֹ: כדוַיֹּ֨אמֶר אֵלָ֤יו יְהוָֹה֙ לֶךְ־רֵ֔ד וְעָלִ֥יתָ אַתָּ֖ה וְאַהֲרֹ֣ן עִמָּ֑ךְ וְהַכֹּהֲנִ֣ים וְהָעָ֗ם אַל־יֶֽהֶרְס֛וּ לַעֲלֹ֥ת אֶל־יְהוָֹ֖ה פֶּן־יִפְרָץ־בָּֽם: כהוַיֹּ֤אמֶר אֵלָ֤יו יְהוָֹה֙ לֶךְ־רֵ֔ד וְעָלִ֥יתָ אַתָּ֖ה וְאַהֲרֹ֣ן עִמָּ֑ךְ וְהַכֹּהֲנִ֣ים וְהָעָ֗ם אַל־יֶֽהֶרְס֛וּ לַעֲלֹ֥ת אֶל־יְהוָֹ֖ה פֶּן־יִפְרָץ־בָּֽם: כהוַיֵּ֥רֶד מֹשֶׁ֖ה אֶל־הָעָ֑ם וַיֹּ֖אמֶר אֲלֵהֶֽם: {ס}

רֵ֖ד הָעֵ֣ד בָּעָ֑ם פֶּן־יֶהֶרְס֤וּ אֶל־יְהוָֹה֙ לִרְאֹ֔ת

Go down, warn the people lest they break [their formation to go nearer] to the Lord, to see

The only hope for the morally right deed in the exceptional case lies in the acknowledgment of universal values and principles that are affirmed and proved by the exception. In a book on the Maquis, Alexander Miller discusses the moral problems with which the underground fighters were confronted in France. Was it permissible for them to forge, to steal, to kill? The response was, "Yes, everything is permitted – and everything is forbidden." What did he mean? The very asking of the question and the recognition that everything was forbidden meant that the Maquis were aware of "code ethics" as a rule, and acknowledged it. But this was an exceptional situation. There were vast and often overwhelming issues and considerations involved. There was no other way to meet those higher considerations than by breaking the rule. One knew that one broke a rule; it was with the necessary sense of the tragic, in a situation of great moral tension, after a great deal of heart-searching. Thus the Maquis. From the angle of the New Morality one would look at it differently. An action as such is neither permitted nor forbidden, only the situation determines right or wrong. When the Maquis kill, there is no confrontation with conscience. There is no advance ruling

FOURTH ALIYAH

[20] The Lord descended upon Mount Sinai, to the peak of the mountain, and the Lord summoned Moses to the peak of the mountain, and Moses ascended. [21] The Lord said to Moses, "**Go down, warn the people lest they break [their formation to go nearer] to the Lord, to see**, and many of them will fall. [22] And also, the priests who go near to the Lord shall prepare themselves, lest the Lord wreak destruction upon them." [23] And Moses said to the Lord, "The people cannot ascend to Mount Sinai, for You warned us saying, 'Set boundaries for the mountain and sanctify it.'" [24] But the Lord said to him, "Go, descend, and [then] you shall ascend, and Aaron with you, but the priests and the populace shall not break [their formation] to ascend to the Lord, lest He wreak destruction upon them." [25] So Moses went down to the people and said [this] to them.

---

that 'thou shalt not kill,' to which a serious measure of consideration is due. The situation rules *ab novo* and spontaneously, thou shalt kill. One prefers the attitude of the underground fighter who realized that what he was doing was a tragic necessity. It is this sense of the tragic that originates in the confrontation between a conscience and an objectively valid norm, which alone lends moral dignity to the deed. It is the only extant safeguard against the inadequacies of human nature. If at times it becomes unavoidable to take a life, woe unto man if he does it without realizing that the rule is "thou shalt not kill," and fails to try to justify his action in the searching and accusing light of that rule. Only the full realization of what ought to be, the heart-searching confrontation with the principle, will – where nothing else is meaningfully possible – lend the quality and the dignity of the moral and the right to the breaking of the universal principle.

In truth, the New Morality itself is a symptom of the collapse of standards and of the spiritual exhaustion of Western civilization that we have analyzed. The tablets of the law are shattered and there is nothing left but love. Love is, of course, a noble ideal. Unfortunately, man is not yet ready to be able to base on it either his own life or the structure of human society.

Crisis and Faith, pages 28–29

שמות פרק כ – עשרת הדברות

אוַיְדַבֵּ֣ר אֱלֹהִ֔ים אֵ֛ת כָּל־הַדְּבָרִ֥ים הָאֵ֖לֶּה לֵאמֹֽר: {ס} בּאָֽנֹכִ֖י יְהֹוָ֣ה
אֱלֹהֶ֑יךָ אֲשֶׁ֧ר הֽוֹצֵאתִ֛יךָ מֵאֶ֥רֶץ מִצְרַ֖יִם מִבֵּ֣ית עֲבָדִ֑ים: גלֹֽא־יִהְיֶ֥ה־לְךָ֛
אֱלֹהִ֥ים אֲחֵרִ֖ים עַל־פָּנָֽי: דלֹֽא־תַֽעֲשֶׂה־לְךָ֥ פֶ֣סֶל | וְכָל־תְּמוּנָ֡ה אֲשֶׁ֣ר
בַּשָּׁמַ֣יִם | מִמַּ֡עַל וַֽאֲשֶׁ֣ר בָּאָ֣רֶץ֩ מִתַּ֨חַת וַֽאֲשֶׁ֧ר בַּמַּ֣יִם | מִתַּ֣חַת לָאָ֑רֶץ: הלֹֽא־
תִשְׁתַּֽחֲוֶ֥ה לָהֶ֖ם וְלֹ֣א תָֽעָבְדֵ֑ם כִּ֣י אָֽנֹכִ֞י יְהֹוָ֤ה אֱלֹהֶ֨יךָ֙ אֵ֣ל קַנָּ֔א פֹּ֠קֵ֣ד עֲוֹ֨ן

וַיְדַבֵּ֣ר אֱלֹהִ֔ים אֵ֛ת כָּל־הַדְּבָרִ֥ים הָאֵ֖לֶּה לֵאמֹֽר

God spoke all these words, saying

The Rabbis in the Talmud and Midrash had the right appreciation of
the nature of the Biblical encounter. We read, for instance, in the Talmud that Rabbi Joshua, the son of Levi, explained: "At the impact of
each word at Sinai, their souls left the Israelites. For so we read, 'My
soul failed me when he spoke' (Daniel, 10:10–11). But if their souls
departed at the first Word, how could they receive the next one? – God
brought down on them the dew with which He will quicken the dead
and thus, revive them. For so does the Psalmist declare, 'A bounteous
rain didst Thou pour down, O God; when Thine inheritance was weary,
Thou didst confirm it'" (Song of Songs, 5:6). According to the Bible,
and to Biblical tradition, man can indeed not endure the encounter
with God. It is true, as Buber says, that in revelation man is revealed to
himself; but in the exact opposite sense in which Buber understands it.
It is man's nothingness that is first revealed to him in the presence of
God. He cannot but realize that, in his own right, he is indeed but "dust
and ashes." He is not annihilated, but he is at the brink of nothingness.
He is brought back into existence by the love of God. His I is returned
to him as a gift of God.

Major Themes in Modern Philosophies of Judaism, page 107

EXODUS CHAPTER 20 – THE DECALOGUE

God spoke all these words, saying: ²"I am the Lord, your God, Who took you out of the land of Egypt, out of the house of bondage. ³You shall not have any **other gods in My presence.** ⁴You shall not make for yourself a graven image or any likeness which is in the heavens above, which is on the earth below, or which is in the water beneath the earth. ⁵You shall neither prostrate yourself before them nor worship them, for I, the Lord, your God, am a zealous God, Who visits the iniquity of the fathers upon the sons, upon the third

---

other gods in My presence　　　　אֱלֹהִים אֲחֵרִים עַל־פָּנַי

We may recall that when the children of Israel made the Golden Calf, they said: This is your Elohim, Israel, who brought you up out of the land of Egypt, and they proceeded to celebrate a feast unto Y (Hashem). Y (Hashem) was the Supreme God, but His was not the menial task of leading people out of the house of bondage. That task He delegated to an Elohim. To counter such ideas the Decalogue commences with the majestic statement: I the omnipotent and transcendent Y (Hashem) am also yours, your Elohim, I am the very same that has brought thee out of Egypt. To bring people out of the house of bondage is also one of my functions. For Y (Hashem) He is Elohim. Therefore, thou shalt have no other Elohim "before me," in addition to my presence, an Elohim to mediate between Me and My creation, between Me and man. The phrase, no other Elohim before Me, conforms to the phrase, which we have discussed earlier, there is none else beside Me.

Hosea put it this way:

"Yet I am Y (Hashem) your Elohim, from the land of Egypt; And you know no Elohim but Me, And beside Me there is no savior" (13:4).

The passage brings to clear expression the identity between Elohim and the savior. However, there is no savior beside Y (Hashem), for Y (Hashem) is Elohim. Israel should have known that since the days of its liberation from Egypt.

Man and God, page 28

אָבֹת עַל־בָּנִים עַל־שִׁלֵּשִׁים וְעַל־רִבֵּעִים לְשֹׂנְאָי: יוְעֹשֶׂה חֶסֶד לַאֲלָפִּים לְאֹהֲבַי וּלְשֹׁמְרֵי מִצְוֹתָי: יֹלֹא תִשָּׂא אֶת־שֵׁם־יְהוָֹה אֱלֹהֶיךָ לַשָּׁוְא כִּי לֹא יְנַקֶּה יְהוָֹה אֵת אֲשֶׁר־יִשָּׂא אֶת־שְׁמוֹ לַשָּׁוְא: יֹזָכוֹר אֶת־יוֹם הַשַּׁבָּת לְקַדְּשׁוֹ: יֹשֵׁשֶׁת יָמִים תַּעֲבֹד וְעָשִׂיתָ כָּל־מְלַאכְתֶּךָ: יֹוְיוֹם הַשְּׁבִיעִי שַׁבָּת

וְעֹשֶׂה חֶסֶד לַאֲלָפִּים   and [I] perform loving kindness to thousands

Let us now see what is the more complete truth about "the forbidding aspect of God as Power," the "incongruous Israelitish concept and service of the 'Jealous God' Yahweh." It seems that Mr. Toynbee himself does not feel comfortable in the strait jacket of his theory. In an annex he makes a partial withdrawal of what he teaches in Volumes VI and VII of his Study. There he concedes that it was not through Jesus that Jewish souls received the first intimation that God is Love. "The Mosaic presentation of Yahweh as a Jealous God, readily moved to anger, had been supplemented by the Prophetic presentation of Him as abounding in mercy and lovingkindness seven hundred years before the Christian Gospel was first preached." Such a confession of itself invalidates the Toynbean position concerning the Israelitish Jealous God. But it is noteworthy that Mr. Toynbee can find no more adequate phrase to describe the Prophetic presentation of God than "abounding in mercy and lovingkindness" – which phrase is itself Mosaic. It was Moses to whom God revealed Himself as: "The Lord, the Lord God, merciful and gracious, long-suffering, and abundant in loving-kindness and truth; keeping mercy unto the thousandth generation, forgiving iniquity and transgression and sin" (Exodus 34:6). The Authorized Version has "goodness" instead of "loving-kindness." The Hebrew *Hesed* is better rendered however with "love and kindness." The two commandments – "Thou shalt love the Lord thy God with all thy heart, and with all thy soul, and with all thy might" and "Thou shalt love thy neighbor as thyself" – are not part of the prophetic presentation but are found in the books of Moses, closely linked to the Jealous God; and yet Jesus said of them: "On these two commandments hang all the law and the

and the fourth generation of those who hate Me, ⁶ **and [I] perform loving kindness to thousands** [of generations], to those who love Me and to those who keep My commandments. ⁷ **You shall not take the name of the Lord, your God, in vain,** for the Lord will not hold blameless anyone who takes His name in vain. ⁸ Remember the Sabbath day to sanctify it. ⁹ Six days may you work and perform all

prophets." There must be something essentially right about a "Jealous God" who admonishes His worshipers: "And if a stranger sojourn with thee in your land, ye shall not do him wrong. The stranger that sojourneth with you shall be unto you as the home-born among you, and thou shalt love him as thyself…" (See Deuteronomy 6:5 and Leviticus 19:18 and 33. Also Matthew 22:40).

Judaism; Fossil or Ferment, pages 55–56

לֹא תִשָּׂא אֶת־שֵׁם־יְהֹוָה אֱלֹהֶיךָ לַשָּׁוְא

You shall not take the name of the Lord, your God, in vain

The wicked seek to prevail by physical might. But there is a divine strategy in history that will not allow them ultimately to triumph. In the end, it will be those who stumbled because they were unable to withstand the violent force which assailed them who will be girded by a strength of a different order and will be saved. Similarly, when David meets Goliath he says to him:

"Thou comest to me with a sword, and with a spear, and with a javelin; but I come to thee in the name of the Lord of Hosts, the God of the armies of Israel, whom thou has taunted…that all this assembly may know that the Lord saves not with sword and spear…" (Samuel 17:45–47).

It is always God on whom one relies, as the Psalmist also puts it:
"For I trust not in my bow,
Neither can my sword save me.
But Thou hast saved us from our adversaries,
And hast put them to shame that hate us" (Psalms 44:7–8).

With God in Hell, page 140

לַיהֹוָ֣ה אֱלֹהֶ֗יךָ לֹֽא־תַעֲשֶׂ֣ה כָל־מְלָאכָ֡ה אַתָּ֣ה וּבִנְךָֽ־וּבִתֶּ֡ךָ עַבְדְּךָ֣ |
וַאֲמָֽתְךָ֩ וּבְהֶמְתֶּ֨ךָ וְגֵרְךָ֜ אֲשֶׁ֣ר בִּשְׁעָרֶ֗יךָ יא כִּ֣י שֵֽׁשֶׁת־יָמִים֩ עָשָׂ֨ה יְהֹוָ֜ה
אֶת־הַשָּׁמַ֣יִם וְאֶת־הָאָ֗רֶץ אֶת־הַיָּם֙ וְאֶת־כָּל־אֲשֶׁר־בָּ֔ם וַיָּ֖נַח בַּיּ֣וֹם הַשְּׁבִיעִ֑י
עַל־כֵּ֗ן בֵּרַ֧ךְ יְהֹוָ֛ה אֶת־י֥וֹם הַשַּׁבָּ֖ת וַֽיְקַדְּשֵֽׁהוּ: יב כַּבֵּ֥ד אֶת־אָבִ֖יךָ וְאֶת־
אִמֶּ֑ךָ לְמַ֙עַן֙ יַֽאֲרִכֻ֣ן יָמֶ֔יךָ עַ֚ל הָֽאֲדָמָ֔ה אֲשֶׁר־יְהֹוָ֥ה אֱלֹהֶ֖יךָ נֹתֵ֥ן לָֽךְ:

---

you shall perform no work   לֹ֣א תַעֲשֶׂ֣ה כָל־מְלָאכָ֡ה

The term "halachic Judaism" needs some explanation. It is not to be understood as a form of Judaism that is opposed to agadic Judaism, a distinction propagated by some authors. There is no such thing as agadic Judaism. Halacha and aggadah are intrinsically interrelated. The great halachists of the Talmud are also the great aggadists. I use the term "halachic Judaism" based on my understanding of the meaning and function of halacha. Halacha is the bridge over which the Torah moves from the written word into the living deed. Normally, there is a confrontation between the text, which is set, and life, which is forever in motion. Even such an apparently easily understood commandment as "Thou shalt do no manner of work on the Sabbath day" requires a lengthy explanation. There is an obvious need to define what is meant by "work." As soon as one undertakes that task, he is involved in the confrontation between a real-life situation and a text. There are innumerable possibilities for human behavior and action, innumerable human needs, and problems arising from them. How to apply to them the specific definition of "work" requires further explanation and interpretation. How to face the confrontation between the text and the actual life situation, how to resolve the problems arising out of this confrontation, is the task of the *Torah sheb'al peh*, the Oral Law. This second Torah, ever since the days of Moses, handed down from generation to generation, accompanies the *Torah shebiktav*, the Written Word, along its journey of realization in the innumerable concrete situations through which the Jewish people pass in the course of its history. It is the wisdom of Torah implementation in the daily life of the Jewish people. It makes the Torah a *Torat chayim*, a living, teaching, and relevant law.

Not in Heaven, Introduction

your labor, [10] but the seventh day is a Sabbath to the Lord, your God; **you shall perform no work**, neither you, your son, your daughter, your manservant, your maidservant, your beast, nor your stranger who is in your cities. [11] For [in] six days the Lord made the heaven and the earth, the sea and all that is in them, and He rested on the seventh day. Therefore, **the Lord blessed the Sabbath day and sanctified it.** [12] Honor your father and your mother, in order that your days be lengthened on the land **that the Lord, your God, is giving you.**

בֵּרַךְ יְהֹוָה אֶת־יוֹם הַשַּׁבָּת וַיְקַדְּשֵׁהוּ
the Lord blessed the Sabbath day and sanctified it

Within Judaism the sacred and the profane are not dialectically related. One might say that within Judaism the sacred, as far as it may be a human concern at all, is not found in the realm of Being, but in that of Becoming. The sacred is not, but must be brought into being as the result of someone's action or behavior. The seventh day is not holy, but becomes holy when God sanctifies it. Israel is made holy by God and becomes holy by sanctifying itself. "Thou shalt be unto Me a kingdom of priests and a holy nation" is not a divine promise of other-worldly transfiguration and redemption, but a challenge to Israel, a task, a responsibility. Man is called upon to sanctify himself; to sanctify this earthly Adam in this world. *Kedusha*, holiness, is sanctification. And sanctification is a process in time and not a miracle outside of time. One is called upon to sanctify one's earthly life.

Faith After the Holocaust, pages 57–58

that the Lord, your God, is giving you   אֲשֶׁר־יְהֹוָה אֱלֹהֶיךָ נֹתֵן לָךְ

Traditionally the laws (*halachot*) of Judaism are divided into two main groups: One contains the laws ordering relationships between man and his fellow; the other, those of a purely ritual nature, as between man and God. At the same time, as is well known, the law of God in the system of Judaism is extremely ramified: It embraces the entire life of the Jew. Man in time and in space, man in society, and man in the world are the subjects of the law. The rhythm of the day and of the week, of the year and of the years, is determined by numerous regulations concerning times of prayer and rest, times set aside for holiday observances. The

יֹּלֹא תִּרְצָח: ס לֹא תִּנְאָף: ס לֹא תִּגְנֹב: ס לֹא־תַעֲנֶה בְרֵעֲךָ עֵד שָׁקֶר:
יֹּדלֹא תַחְמֹד בֵּית רֵעֶךָ ס לֹא־תַחְמֹד אֵשֶׁת רֵעֶךָ וְעַבְדּוֹ וַאֲמָתוֹ וְשׁוֹרוֹ
וַחֲמֹרוֹ וְכֹל אֲשֶׁר לְרֵעֶךָ:

---

law also prescribes one's dealings with the world of things about us by the many rules about foods to eat and not to eat, clothing to wear and not to wear. The pursuit of the building of a home has its respective observances. And, needless to say, the same is true of man's intercourse with his fellow man in society or in the family, in the state, and among the nations. All are circumscribed by the law. Every important event in the life of the Jew is brought under the dominion of the law. There seems to be no niche or nook into which the law has not penetrated. The law is present all the time and everywhere. The Jew is indeed surrounded by *mitzvot* on all sides.

God, Man and History, pages 91–92

You shall not murder   לֹא תִּרְצָח

The universe cannot be dismissed that simply – and certainly not after the Holocaust. It is true that nowhere on earth and never before in history could one experience the absurdity of existence as in the German death camps; but it is also true that nowhere else in this world and never before could one experience the nobility of existence as there and then. And the one is not unrelated to the other. At Auschwitz and Treblinka, in the camps and the ghettos, man sank to his lowest level yet, but there too he was exalted to his highest dignity. The story of man's degradation is well known. Perhaps, in our sorrow over it, we have paid little attention to the greatness of man. Let a few examples stand here for what we mean by the experience of the nobility of existence even next door to the crematoria. One of the survivors of the Warsaw Ghetto tells the story of how he and a woman were sought by the Gestapo. They were chased for weeks, living continually under the shadow of imminent death, changing their hiding place from day to day, until finally they were trapped behind the accumulated garbage of a ghetto attic. The man was determined to sell his life dearly. As the policeman approached his corner, he jumped forward and got him by the throat. The policeman went limp in his hand, completely at his

¹³**You shall not murder**. You shall not commit adultery. You shall not steal. You shall not bear false witness against your neighbor. ¹⁴**You shall not covet** your neighbor's house. You shall not covet your neighbor's wife, his manservant, his maidservant, his ox, his donkey, or whatever belongs to your neighbor."

---

mercy. At this moment, "Sonya ran from her hiding place and shouted hysterically: Don't kill him! Don't kill him!" What manifestation of human dignity in this Jewish woman, who after having been stalked by death for weeks, becomes hysterical at the thought that her companion in hiding should kill their pursuer! And the vaster the inhumanity that surrounds her on all sides, the more awe-inspiring is the nobility of existence that she exemplifies. At that moment there was no place on earth holier than that dark and dusty corner in that attic in the Warsaw Ghetto. It was the Holy of Holies on earth, sharing in the very majesty of Sinai, when God, descending upon it, proclaimed His "Thou shalt not kill!" Who knows whether that wretched little attic was not wrapped in even greater majesty than Sinai! At Sinai God proclaimed; in the ghetto a hunted human being, at the risk of her own life, enacted God's commandment.

Faith After the Holocaust, pages 76–77

You shall not covet   לֹא תַחְמֹד

The ethical significance of the two categories of "ritual" laws, which we have been discussing, consists in that they ready the biophysical organism, the only means of ethical conduct, for effective ethical action by setting up the classical training situation. Any one commandment of the Decalogue, "you shall not commit adultery" or "you shall not kill" or "you shall not covet" – is an ethical injunction directed to a real situation of conflict or temptation. In order to obey it, one must inhibit powerfully aroused passions. But one does not learn the art of self-control by merely reading the Bible. One learns it by actually controlling oneself in the face of a challenge. However, when the challenge actually arises in all seriousness, it may be too late to inhibit and act ethically and effectively. To delay one's preparations for meeting the challenge until it actually presents itself would be the direct method, which usually leads to failure. The direct attack on the amoral and, perhaps, even anti-moral

חמישי

טו וְכָל־הָעָם רֹאִים אֶת־הַקּוֹלֹת וְאֶת־הַלַּפִּידִם וְאֵת קוֹל הַשֹּׁפָר וְאֶת־הָהָר
עָשֵׁן וַיַּרְא הָעָם וַיָּנֻעוּ וַיַּעַמְדוּ מֵרָחֹק: טז וַיֹּאמְרוּ אֶל־מֹשֶׁה דַּבֶּר־אַתָּה
עִמָּנוּ וְנִשְׁמָעָה וְאַל־יְדַבֵּר עִמָּנוּ אֱלֹהִים פֶּן־נָמוּת: יז וַיֹּאמֶר מֹשֶׁה אֶל־הָעָם

---

egocentricity of the physical organism is as unwise an undertaking as
the sending of untrained recruits into the firing line. Emotions will be
mastered only by stronger emotions. The dynamic charge of vital urges
will be held in check by the more potent charge of opposing and no less
vital desires. But, originally, the desire for the good, as one of the vital
urges within human nature, is outnumbered by opposing forces.

God, Man and History, pages 113–114

And all the people saw the voices   וְכָל־הָעָם רֹאִים אֶת־הַקּוֹלֹת

The covenant is the most intense form of the encounter. But the encounter must be real for me, or else it does not exist for me; and so it is
with the covenant too. The covenant with my ancestors was concluded
with them. As an event in history, it could not but affect the lives of
their children as well; yet it could not be a covenant with the children.
For me it is history, not encounter, that my forefathers encountered
God. However, where there is no encounter, there may be philosophiz-
ing about religion, but there is no religion. For the revelation at Sinai to
be revelation for me, it must be addressed to me. And so the covenant
had to be concluded with all generations.

This could be done because, while the generations of the wilderness
did pass away, God is timeless, and therefore the manifestation at Sinai
is timelessly directed to Israel. The revelation at Sinai never belongs
to the past; it never ceases to be. It is as if the Divine Presence, never
departing from the mountain, were waiting for each new generation
to come to Sinai to encounter it and to receive the word. Judged from
the aspect of God's relationship to Israel, as revealed at Sinai or in
the exodus from Egypt, these encounters are ever-present events. The
miracles and the signs, the thunder and the lightning are gone; but not
God, or the message, or Israel. And so it is for the eye of faith to see
what has been withdrawn from the senses and for the ear of faith to
hear, notwithstanding the silence. The idea has been expressed in many

Fifth Aliyah

[15] **And all the people saw the voices** and the torches, the sound of the shofar, and the smoking mountain, and the people saw and trembled; so they stood from afar. [16] They said to Moses, "**You speak with us, and we will hear**, but let God not speak with us lest we

---

variations in talmudic and midrashic literature. According to Mishna Avot 6:2, "Every day a heavenly voice goes forth from Mount Sinai." Various verses in the Bible are interpreted by the rabbis as enjoining Jews that the Torah should be for them as if it were given from Sinai today (Brachot 63b; see also Yalkut Shimoni on Deuteronomy 26).

God, Man and History, page 44

You speak with us, and we will hear   דַּבֵּר־אַתָּה עִמָּנוּ וְנִשְׁמָעָה

The past cannot be called back, and moreover it should not be called back. The great rabbinical personalities of the past are not the men to solve the problems of modern Jewries. We can hardly make any greater mistake than to call in the old type of Gaon of the Russian or Polish Jewries to assist us in our difficulties. The new situation demands new men. They must be men who themselves are children of this new situation. They must themselves have suffered all the agonies of the dualism in the life of the modern Jew. The conflict of the two worlds must have torn their own hearts and minds, without this they cannot realize how genuine and serious the problems are, nor begin to seek a remedy. As long as the present period of transition lasts, it is vital that leadership should grow from the great spiritual travail in the clash of the two civilizations. This can only happen where men actually live in the two worlds. Living in two worlds obviates one-sidedness in two respects. It obviates the one-sidedness of a rabbinical authority rooted in the past, and the one-sidedness of exclusive attachment to Western European civilization. Neither the Gaon of yesterday nor the *Am ha' Aretz* of today is the man we need. The rabbi who is fitted for authority and leadership today in Jewry must be deeply rooted in both historic Judaism and modern European civilization. He must be a *Talmid Chacham* and a scientist, philosopher or historian in one. Europe and Sinai should meet in his soul. And only so far as he is able to maintain his

אַל־תִּירָאוּ כִּי לְבַעֲבוּר נַסּוֹת אֶתְכֶם בָּא הָאֱלֹהִים וּבַעֲבוּר תִּהְיֶה יִרְאָתוֹ עַל־פְּנֵיכֶם לְבִלְתִּי תֶחֱטָאוּ: יחוַיַּעֲמֹד הָעָם מֵרָחֹק וּמֹשֶׁה נִגַּשׁ אֶל־הָעֲרָפֶל אֲשֶׁר־שָׁם הָאֱלֹהִים: יטוַיֹּאמֶר יְהֹוָה אֶל־מֹשֶׁה כֹּה תֹאמַר אֶל־בְּנֵי יִשְׂרָאֵל אַתֶּם רְאִיתֶם כִּי מִן־הַשָּׁמַיִם דִּבַּרְתִּי עִמָּכֶם: כלֹא תַעֲשׂוּן אִתִּי אֱלֹהֵי כֶסֶף וֵאלֹהֵי זָהָב לֹא תַעֲשׂוּ לָכֶם: כאמִזְבַּח אֲדָמָה תַּעֲשֶׂה־לִּי וְזָבַחְתָּ עָלָיו אֶת־ עֹלֹתֶיךָ וְאֶת־שְׁלָמֶיךָ אֶת־צֹאנְךָ וְאֶת־בְּקָרֶךָ בְּכָל־הַמָּקוֹם אֲשֶׁר אַזְכִּיר אֶת־שְׁמִי אָבוֹא אֵלֶיךָ וּבֵרַכְתִּיךָ: כבוְאִם־מִזְבַּח אֲבָנִים תַּעֲשֶׂה־לִּי לֹא־ תִבְנֶה אֶתְהֶן גָּזִית כִּי חַרְבְּךָ הֵנַפְתָּ עָלֶיהָ וַתְּחַלְלֶהָ: כגוְלֹא־תַעֲלֶה בְמַעֲלֹת עַל־מִזְבְּחִי אֲשֶׁר לֹא־תִגָּלֶה עֶרְוָתְךָ עָלָיו:

Judaism in his own personal experience of the conflict will he be able to give guidance to Jewry today. Only a personality harmonized within itself, after a struggle of conflicting ideas, will be able to reveal the message of Judaism to this generation, for such alone will be in a position to translate it into the terms of our century.

Such an achievement demands knowledge and character; real knowledge of Judaism combined with critical insight into the structure and working of Western civilization, and a character that is strong enough to bear the strain of leaving many problems unsolved, strong enough to think sincerely while deliberate in translating thought into act, cautious and yet bold.

Towards Historic Judaism, pages 109–110

die." [17] But Moses said to the people, "Fear not, for God has come in order to exalt you, and in order that His awe shall be upon your faces, so that you shall not sin." [18] The people remained far off, but Moses drew near to the opaque darkness, where God was. [19] The Lord said to Moses, "So shall you say to the children of Israel, You have seen that from the heavens I have spoken with you. [20] You shall not make [images of anything that is] with Me. Gods of silver or gods of gold you shall not make for yourselves. [21] An altar of earth you shall make for Me, and you shall slaughter beside it your burnt offerings and your peace offerings, your sheep and your cattle. **Wherever I allow My name to be mentioned, I will come to you and bless you**. [22] And when you make for Me an altar of stones, you shall not build them of hewn stones, lest you wield your sword upon it and desecrate it. [23] And you shall not ascend with steps upon My altar, so that your nakedness shall not be exposed upon it."

בְּכָל־הַמָּקוֹם אֲשֶׁר אַזְכִּיר אֶת־שְׁמִי אָבוֹא אֵלֶיךָ וּבֵרַכְתִּיךָ

Wherever I allow My name to be mentioned, I will come to you and bless you

It is to be noted that whenever God's "holy habitation" is mentioned in the Bible, often identical with the heavens, it is the "place" from which God turns toward man, knowing him and considering him.

In Deuteronomy, we read the prayer:

"Look forth from the habitation of Thy holiness, from heaven, and bless Thy people Israel, and the land which Thou hast given us, as Thou didst swear unto our fathers" (26:15).

God's "holy habitation" is not what sets God and man apart; it is the point from which his blessings are expected. God relates himself to his people by blessing them and their land.

Man and God, page 171

מפטיר

במדבר פרק כח

כּוּבְיוֹם הַבִּכּוּרִים בְּהַקְרִיבְכֶם מִנְחָה חֲדָשָׁה לַיהוָה בְּשָׁבֻעֹתֵיכֶם מִקְרָא־קֹדֶשׁ יִהְיֶה לָכֶם כָּל־מְלֶאכֶת עֲבֹדָה לֹא תַעֲשׂוּ: כּזוְהִקְרַבְתֶּם עוֹלָה לְרֵיחַ נִיחֹחַ לַיהוָה פָּרִים בְּנֵי־בָקָר שְׁנַיִם אַיִל אֶחָד שִׁבְעָה כְבָשִׂים בְּנֵי שָׁנָה: כּחוּמִנְחָתָם סֹלֶת בְּלוּלָה בַשָּׁמֶן שְׁלֹשָׁה עֶשְׂרֹנִים לַפָּר הָאֶחָד שְׁנֵי עֶשְׂרֹנִים לָאַיִל הָאֶחָד: כּטעִשָּׂרוֹן עִשָּׂרוֹן לַכֶּבֶשׂ הָאֶחָד לְשִׁבְעַת הַכְּבָשִׂים: לְשָׂעִיר עִזִּים אֶחָד לְכַפֵּר עֲלֵיכֶם: לֹאמִלְּבַד עֹלַת הַתָּמִיד וּמִנְחָתוֹ תַּעֲשׂוּ תְּמִימִם יִהְיוּ־לָכֶם וְנִסְכֵּיהֶם:

| first fruits | הַבִּכּוּרִים |

"And it shall be, when you come in unto the land which the Lord thy God gives you for an inheritance, and possess it, and dwell therein, that thou shall take of the first of all the fruit of the ground ... and thou shall put it in a basket, and shalt go unto the place which the Lord thy God shall choose to cause His name to dwell there" (Deuteronomy 26:1–2).

Naturally, this commandment, which was the expression of the gratitude of the people for the good land which God gave them, could only be fulfilled in the land, after Israel had taken possession of the land. As the Talmud remarks: "The commandment of the first fruits was not binding before the land had been conquered and divided among the tribes of Israel." In view of this, the comment in the Midrash is rather surprising: "Do this commandment, for in the merit of its fulfillment you will enter the land." The question is rightly asked: How could the observance of this commandment help the Israelites to enter the land if the prior condition of the "first fruits" was the possession of the land? How could the Israelites fulfill the commandment of the "first fruits" outside the land and before its conquest?

This is not merely an academic question, concerning a practice which has been in abeyance for thousands of years. The answer to it contains a deep significance for ourselves at the present moment. It would be possible to apply this thought in general, to the present world-struggle, but we will confine ourselves here to an important aspect of Jewish life on which the Midrash we have quoted may throw some light.

Maftir Aliyah
Numbers Chapter 28

²⁶ And on the day of the **first fruits**, when you offer up a new meal offering to the Lord, on your festival of Weeks; it shall be a holy convocation for you, and you shall not perform any mundane work. ²⁷ You shall offer up a burnt offering with a spirit of satisfaction to the Lord: two young bulls, one ram, and seven lambs in the first year. ²⁸ Their meal offerings [shall be] fine flour mixed with oil; three-tenths for each bull and two-tenths for the ram. ²⁹ One-tenth for each lamb, for all seven lambs. ³⁰ One young male goat to atone for you. ³¹ You shall offer this up besides the continual burnt offering and its meal offering they shall be unblemished for you, as well as their libations.

The Jewish nation and our communities are confronted with innumerable tasks today. All the old foundations of Jewish life have disappeared. We have to rebuild Judaism, both materially and spiritually, all over the world. All over the world, I say, and not only in Poland or Germany or Rumania; here too, in this country (England) and in America and in Australia – everywhere. There is chaos everywhere, and not only in the occupied countries of Europe. There is chaos here and in America. There is chaos in our communal organizations, chaos in our religious life, in Jewish education, in our national aspirations, chaos in the heart and the mind of the modern Jew, chaos or emptiness. Wherever you turn, there is always the same lack of principle, the same lack of knowledge and humility. But when you point in detail to the sore spots in Jewish life, when you suggest certain remedies, when you ask for something that should be done, the usual answer is: there is a war on, we must wait, first we must conquer the promised land, then we shall offer "first fruits." Jews think that Judaism can hibernate for the duration. We postpone Judaism and do not realize that from Judaism alone can we derive the strength that we need to survive and to enter the promised land.

Most of these "there is a war on" replies, when urgent and vital tasks of Jewish life demand our attention, are but the excuses of laziness and self-indulgence, of irresponsibility and indifference. Now, if ever, is the time for deepening Jewish consciousness, for spreading Jewish knowledge, for safeguarding traditional Jewish life, and for planning

הפטרה

יחזקאל פרק א

וַיְהִי | בִּשְׁלֹשִׁים שָׁנָה בָּרְבִיעִי בַּחֲמִשָּׁה לַחֹדֶשׁ וַאֲנִי בְתוֹךְ־הַגּוֹלָה עַל־נְהַר־כְּבָר נִפְתְּחוּ הַשָּׁמַיִם וָאֶרְאֶה מַרְאוֹת אֱלֹהִים: בַּחֲמִשָּׁה לַחֹדֶשׁ הִיא הַשָּׁנָה הַחֲמִישִׁית לְגָלוּת הַמֶּלֶךְ יוֹיָכִין: הָיֹה הָיָה דְבַר־יְהֹוָה אֶל־יְחֶזְקֵאל בֶּן־בּוּזִי הַכֹּהֵן בְּאֶרֶץ כַּשְׂדִּים עַל־נְהַר־כְּבָר וַתְּהִי עָלָיו שָׁם יַד־יְהֹוָה: וָאֵרֶא וְהִנֵּה רוּחַ סְעָרָה בָּאָה מִן־הַצָּפוֹן עָנָן גָּדוֹל וְאֵשׁ מִתְלַקַּחַת וְנֹגַהּ לוֹ סָבִיב וּמִתּוֹכָהּ כְּעֵין הַחַשְׁמַל מִתּוֹךְ הָאֵשׁ: וּמִתּוֹכָהּ דְּמוּת אַרְבַּע חַיּוֹת וְזֶה מַרְאֵיהֶן דְּמוּת אָדָם לָהֵנָּה: וְאַרְבָּעָה פָנִים לְאֶחָת וְאַרְבַּע כְּנָפַיִם לְאַחַת לָהֶם: וְרַגְלֵיהֶם רֶגֶל יְשָׁרָה וְכַף רַגְלֵיהֶם כְּכַף רֶגֶל עֵגֶל וְנֹצְצִים כְּעֵין נְחֹשֶׁת קָלָל: וְיָדֵי (וידו) אָדָם מִתַּחַת כַּנְפֵיהֶם עַל אַרְבַּעַת רִבְעֵיהֶם

---

and preparing the Jewish future with all our remaining spiritual and material resources. Now and not tomorrow!

Between Yesterday and Tomorrow, pages 127, 130

הָיֹה הָיָה דְבַר־יְהֹוָה אֶל־יְחֶזְקֵאל

The word of the Lord was [revealed] to Ezekiel

Ezekiel 2:2 reads, "and the spirit entered into me when he spoke unto me, and set me upon my feet," and then we find immediately following, the message which was delivered to the prophet. See also Ezekiel 3:24, and especially 11:5, where the spirit which enables the prophet to speak the word of prophecy is called the *ruach Adonai*.

Now as to Ezekiel 2:2 and 3:24, we note first that no mention is made of ruach Y (Hashem). The undetermined *ruach* – a wind, a spirit, a power – occurs. As always in such cases, the meaning must be elicited from the context. Having described his first momentous vision, Ezekiel continues:

Haftarah

Ezekiel Chapter 1

Now it came to pass in the thirtieth year in the fourth [month] on the fifth day of the month, as I was in the midst of the exile by the river Chebar – the heavens opened up, and I saw visions of God. ² "On the fifth of the month" – that is the fifth year of King Jehoiachin's exile. ³ **The word of the Lord was [revealed] to Ezekiel** the son of Buzi, the priest, in the land of the Chaldeans, by the river Chebar, and the hand of the Lord came upon him there. ⁴ And I saw, and behold, a tempest was coming from the north, a huge cloud and a flaming fire with a brightness around it; and from its midst, it was like the color of the chashmal from the midst of the fire. ⁵ And from its midst was the likeness of four living beings, and this is their appearance; they had the likeness of a man. ⁶ And [each] one had four faces, and [each] one had four wings. ⁷ And their legs were a straight leg, and the soles of their feet were like a round foot, and they sparkled like the color of burnished copper. ⁸ And human hands were beneath their wings on

---

This was the appearance of the likeness of the glory of the Y (Hashem). And when I saw, I fell upon my face, and I heard a voice of one that spoke. And He said unto me: "Son of man, stand upon thy feet, and I will speak with thee." And *ruach* entered into me when He spoke unto me, and set me upon my feet; and I heard Him that spoke to me. And He said to me....

Quite clearly the Speaker is not to be identified with the *ruach*. The *ruach* here has nothing to do with the spirit of prophecy. Lying on the ground, Ezekiel hears the Speaker. Even before the ruach enters him, the prophet is being addressed. This is the beginning of the act of prophecy. Even at the moment of the entry of the *ruach*, the *ruach* is distinguished from the Speaker. The *ruach* has only one function. The words of the Speaker: "Son of man, stand upon thy feet" and the subsequent statement that the spirit that entered Ezekiel set him upon his feet give a full indication of that function. Ezekiel's falling upon his face before the vision was not a completely free act of worshiping prostration. He is physically too overwhelmed by his experience. In a condition of complete bodily exhaustion, he lies there on the ground

וּפְנֵיהֶ֖ם וְכַנְפֵיהֶ֣ם לְאַרְבַּעְתָּֽם: טו חֹֽבְרֹ֗ת אִשָּׁה֙ אֶל־אֲחוֹתָ֔הּ כַּנְפֵיהֶ֖ם לֹֽא־יִסַּ֣בּוּ בְלֶכְתָּ֑ן אִ֛ישׁ אֶל־עֵ֥בֶר פָּנָ֖יו יֵלֵֽכוּ: י וּדְמ֣וּת פְּנֵיהֶם֮ פְּנֵ֣י אָדָם֒ וּפְנֵ֨י אַרְיֵ֤ה אֶל־הַיָּמִין֙ לְאַרְבַּעְתָּ֔ם וּפְנֵי־שׁ֥וֹר מֵֽהַשְּׂמֹ֖אל (מהשמאול) לְאַרְבַּעְתָּ֑ן וּפְנֵי־נֶ֖שֶׁר לְאַרְבַּעְתָּֽן: יא וּפְנֵיהֶ֕ם וְכַנְפֵיהֶ֥ם פְּרֻד֖וֹת מִלְמָ֑עְלָה לְאִ֗ישׁ שְׁתַּ֨יִם֙ חֹֽבְר֣וֹת אִ֔ישׁ וּשְׁתַּ֣יִם מְכַסּ֔וֹת אֵ֖ת גְּוִיֹּתֵיהֶֽנָה: יב וְאִ֛ישׁ אֶל־עֵ֥בֶר פָּנָ֖יו יֵלֵ֑כוּ אֶ֣ל אֲשֶׁר֩ יִֽהְיֶה־שָׁ֨מָּה הָר֤וּחַ לָלֶ֨כֶת֙ יֵלֵ֔כוּ לֹ֥א יִסַּ֖בּוּ בְּלֶכְתָּֽן: יג וּדְמ֨וּת הַֽחַיּ֜וֹת מַרְאֵיהֶ֗ם כְּגַֽחֲלֵי־אֵ֤שׁ בֹּֽעֲרוֹת֙ כְּמַרְאֵ֣ה הַלַּפִּדִ֔ים הִ֕יא מִתְהַלֶּ֖כֶת בֵּ֣ין הַֽחַיּ֑וֹת וְנֹ֣גַהּ לָאֵ֔שׁ וּמִן־הָאֵ֖שׁ יוֹצֵ֥א בָרָֽק: יד וְהַֽחַיּ֖וֹת רָצ֣וֹא וָשׁ֑וֹב כְּמַרְאֵ֖ה הַבָּזָֽק: טו וָאֵ֖רֶא הַֽחַיּ֑וֹת וְהִנֵּה֩ אוֹפַ֨ן אֶחָ֥ד בָּאָ֛רֶץ אֵ֥צֶל הַֽחַיּ֖וֹת לְאַרְבַּ֥עַת פָּנָֽיו: טז מַרְאֵ֨ה הָאֽוֹפַנִּ֤ים וּמַֽעֲשֵׂיהֶם֙ כְּעֵ֣ין תַּרְשִׁ֔ישׁ וּדְמ֥וּת אֶחָ֖ד לְאַרְבַּעְתָּ֑ן וּמַרְאֵיהֶם֙ וּמַ֣עֲשֵׂיהֶ֔ם כַּֽאֲשֶׁ֛ר יִֽהְיֶ֥ה הָאוֹפַ֖ן בְּת֥וֹךְ הָאוֹפָֽן: יז עַל־אַרְבַּ֥עַת רִבְעֵיהֶ֖ן בְּלֶכְתָּ֣ם יֵלֵ֑כוּ לֹ֥א יִסַּ֖בּוּ בְּלֶכְתָּֽן: יח וְגַ֨בֵּיהֶ֔ן וְגֹ֥בַהּ לָהֶ֖ם וְיִרְאָ֣ה לָהֶ֑ם וְגַבֹּתָ֗ם מְלֵאֹ֥ת עֵינַ֛יִם סָבִ֖יב לְאַרְבַּעְתָּֽן: יט וּבְלֶ֨כֶת֙ הַֽחַיּ֔וֹת יֵֽלְכ֥וּ הָאֽוֹפַנִּ֖ים אֶצְלָ֑ם וּבְהִנָּשֵׂ֤א הַֽחַיּוֹת֙ מֵעַ֣ל הָאָ֔רֶץ יִנָּֽשְׂא֖וּ הָאֽוֹפַנִּֽים: כ עַ֣ל אֲשֶׁר֩ יִֽהְיֶה־שָּׁ֨ם הָר֤וּחַ לָלֶ֨כֶת֙ יֵלֵ֔כוּ שָׁ֥מָּה הָר֖וּחַ לָלֶ֑כֶת וְהָאֽוֹפַנִּ֗ים יִנָּֽשְׂאוּ֙ לְעֻמָּתָ֔ם כִּ֛י ר֥וּחַ הַֽחַיָּ֖ה בָּאֽוֹפַנִּֽים: כא בְּלֶכְתָּ֣ם יֵלֵ֔כוּ וּבְעָמְדָ֖ם יַֽעֲמֹ֑דוּ וּֽבְהִנָּֽשְׂאָ֞ם מֵעַ֣ל הָאָ֗רֶץ יִנָּֽשְׂא֤וּ הָאֽוֹפַנִּים֙ לְעֻמָּתָ֔ם כִּ֛י ר֥וּחַ הַֽחַיָּ֖ה בָּאֽוֹפַנִּֽים: כב וּדְמ֞וּת עַל־רָאשֵׁ֤י הַֽחַיָּה֙ רָקִ֔יעַ כְּעֵ֖ין הַקֶּ֣רַח הַנּוֹרָ֑א נָט֥וּי עַל־רָֽאשֵׁיהֶ֖ם מִלְמָֽעְלָה: כג וְתַ֨חַת֙ הָֽרָקִ֔יעַ כַּנְפֵיהֶ֖ם יְשָׁר֑וֹת אִשָּׁ֣ה אֶל־אֲחוֹתָ֔הּ לְאִ֗ישׁ שְׁתַּ֤יִם מְכַסּוֹת֙ לָהֵ֔נָּה וּלְאִ֗ישׁ שְׁתַּ֤יִם מְכַסּוֹת֙

(Daniel 10:8) before God. He hears a voice that speaks but he is unable to grasp the message. "Stand up and listen," says the voice, but he has no strength left. The *ruach* enters and sets him up on his feet. The *ruach* restores the prophet's bodily energies. The prophet may now receive the message, and the Speaker that was there all the time and spoke to Ezekiel even before the *ruach* approached, continues with his message. The situation is exactly the same in Ezekiel 3:24. In neither of these cases does *ruach* "control the prophet" nor has it anything to do with the spirit of prophecy.

Man and God, pages 78–79

their four sides, and their faces and their wings were [the same] to all four of them. ⁹Their wings joined one to the other; they did not turn when they walked; each one would go toward the direction of his face. ¹⁰And the likeness of their faces was the face of a man, and the face of a lion was on their right, to the four of them, and the face of an ox to their left, to the four of them, and the face of an eagle [was] to the four of them. ¹¹And so were their faces. And their wings were extended upward; each one had two wings joined to each other, and two covering their bodies. ¹²Now each one would go toward the direction of his face; wherever would be the will to go, they would go; they did not turn as they walked. ¹³And the likeness of the living beings; their appearance was like fiery coals, burning like the appearance of firebrands; it was going among the living beings; and there was a brightness to the fire and from the fire came forth lightning. ¹⁴And the living beings would run and return, like the appearance of the sparks. ¹⁵And I saw the living beings, and behold, one wheel [was] on the ground beside the living beings for its four faces. ¹⁶The appearance of the wheels and their work was like the appearance of crystal, and the four of them had one likeness, and their appearance and their workings were as a wheel would be within a wheel. ¹⁷When they went, they went toward their four sides; they did not turn when they went. ¹⁸And they had backs, and they were very high, and they were dreadful, and their eyebrows were full of eyes round about – [so it was] to the four of them. ¹⁹And when the living beings would go, the wheels would go beside them; and when the living beings would lift themselves off the ground, the wheels would lift themselves. ²⁰Wherever there was the will to go, they would go; there was the will to go, and the wheels would lift themselves correspondingly to them, for the will of the living being was in the wheels. ²¹When they [the living beings] would go, they [the wheels] would go, and when they would stand, they would stand, and when they would lift themselves up from the ground, the wheels would lift themselves correspondingly to them, for the will of the living being was in the wheels. ²²And there was a likeness over the heads of the living beings, of an expanse like the color of the severe frost extended over their heads above. ²³And beneath the expanse, their wings were straight, one [pointed] toward the other; this one had two that covered, to here, and that one had two that covered, to here, their

לְהֵ֫נָּה אֵ֣ת גְּוִיֹּתֵיהֶ֑ם: כדוָאֶשְׁמַ֣ע אֶת־ק֣וֹל כַּנְפֵיהֶ֡ם כְּק֣וֹל מַ֣יִם רַבִּ֣ים כְּקוֹל־
שַׁדַּי֙ בְּלֶכְתָּ֔ם ק֥וֹל הֲמֻלָּ֖ה כְּק֣וֹל מַחֲנֶ֑ה בְּעׇמְדָ֖ם תְּרַפֶּ֥ינָה כַנְפֵיהֶֽן: כהוַיְהִי־
ק֕וֹל מֵעַ֕ל לָרָקִ֖יעַ אֲשֶׁ֣ר עַל־רֹאשָׁ֑ם בְּעׇמְדָ֖ם תְּרַפֶּ֥ינָה כַנְפֵיהֶֽן: כווּמִמַּ֗עַל
לָרָקִ֙יעַ֙ אֲשֶׁ֣ר עַל־רֹאשָׁ֔ם כְּמַרְאֵ֥ה אֶֽבֶן־סַפִּ֖יר דְּמ֣וּת כִּסֵּ֑א וְעַל֙ דְּמ֣וּת הַכִּסֵּ֔א
דְּמ֞וּת כְּמַרְאֵ֥ה אָדָ֛ם עָלָ֖יו מִלְמָֽעְלָה: כזוָאֵ֣רֶא | כְּעֵ֣ין חַשְׁמַ֗ל כְּמַרְאֵה־אֵ֤שׁ
בֵּֽית־לָהּ֙ סָבִ֔יב מִמַּרְאֵ֥ה מׇתְנָ֖יו וּלְמָ֑עְלָה וּמִמַּרְאֵ֤ה מׇתְנָיו֙ וּלְמַ֔טָּה רָאִ֨יתִי֙
כְּמַרְאֵה־אֵ֔שׁ וְנֹ֥גַֽהּ ל֖וֹ סָבִֽיב: כחכְּמַרְאֵ֣ה הַקֶּ֡שֶׁת אֲשֶׁר֩ יִֽהְיֶ֨ה בֶעָנָ֜ן בְּי֣וֹם
הַגֶּ֗שֶׁם כֵּ֣ן מַרְאֵ֤ה הַנֹּ֨גַהּ֙ סָבִ֔יב ה֕וּא מַרְאֵ֖ה דְּמ֣וּת כְּבוֹד־יְהֹוָ֑ה וָֽאֶרְאֶה֙ וָאֶפֹּ֣ל
עַל־פָּנַ֔י וָאֶשְׁמַ֖ע ק֥וֹל מְדַבֵּֽר:

יחזקאל פרק ג

יבוַתִּשָּׂאֵ֣נִי ר֔וּחַ וָאֶשְׁמַ֣ע אַחֲרַ֔י ק֖וֹל רַ֣עַשׁ גָּד֑וֹל בָּר֥וּךְ כְּבוֹד־יְהֹוָ֖ה
מִמְּקוֹמֽוֹ:

I fell on my face	וָאֶפֹּ֣ל עַל־פָּנַ֔י

God, who reveals his "unbearable" Presence to the helpless creature, also sustains man in the act of revelation. The prophet Ezekiel, for instance, reports on one of his encounters: "And I fell on my face. Then the spirit entered into me, and set me upon my feet, and spoke with me…" (3:23–24). The key phrase is "and set me upon my feet." The prophet fell on his face because he was thrown to the ground by the force of the encounter. But in that condition of weakness, his ability as a messenger of God to Israel was taken from him. Only after the spirit had set him on his feet could God address him. The encounter crushed Ezekiel; but it was in the encounter that he was granted the strength to stand up and, notwithstanding the terror, face the Presence. God can meet man only by sustaining him against the impact of God's own Presence.

Obviously, not just any form of life sustained in the prophet will allow the encounter to take place. It is not enough to grant him a kind of life that may make of him some new creation, in the old external

bodies. [24] And I heard the sound of their wings, like the sound of many waters like the voice of the Almighty – when they went; the sound of stirring, like the sound of a camp; when they would stand, they would let down their wings. [25] And there was a voice above the expanse that was over their heads; when they stood still, they would let down their wings. [26] And above the expanse that was over their heads, like the appearance of a sapphire stone, was the likeness of a throne, and on the likeness of the throne, was a likeness like the appearance of a man upon it above. [27] And I saw like the color of chashmal like the appearance of fire within it round about, from the appearance of his loins and above; and from the appearance of his loins and below, I saw [a thing] like the appearance of fire, and there was a brightness round about it. [28] Like the appearance of the rainbow that is in the cloud on a rainy day, so was the appearance of the brightness round about; that was the appearance of the likeness of the glory of the Lord, and when I saw, **I fell on my face**, and I heard a voice speaking.

EZEKIEL CHAPTER 3

[12] And a wind lifted me up, and I heard behind me the sound of a great uproar: "Blessed is the glory of the Lord from His place."

---

garb. The spirit must set Ezekiel on his feet, so that he may again be himself. His own self must be returned to him; otherwise, no encounter with Ezekiel per se is possible.

But Ezekiel may retain his personal identity in the encounter if God, in revealing His presence, protects the prophet against His "consuming" essence. All protection that shields the prophet, however, hides God from him. God can only reveal Himself to man by hiding Himself in the very act of revelation. In the peril, which is implied (and yet restrained) in the encounter, God both reveals and hides Himself. He reveals Himself, that His concern for man may be known; He hides Himself in the very act of revelation so that the subject of his concern will not be consumed by the very knowledge shown to Him. He reveals Himself as a "hiding" God, so that man may live in His sight.

God, Man and History, pages 34–35

קריאת התורה יום שני

בשבת מתחילים בדברים פרק יד:כב-דברים פרק טו:א-יח

בחול מתחילים בדברים פרק טו:יט-טז:יז; מפטיר: במדבר פרק כח:כו-לא:
הפטרה: חבקוק פרק ב:כ-ג:יט (עמוד 124)

ראשון כשחל בשבת
דברים פרק יד

כב עַשֵּׂר תְּעַשֵּׂר אֵת כָּל־תְּבוּאַת זַרְעֶךָ הַיֹּצֵא הַשָּׂדֶה שָׁנָה שָׁנָה: כג וְאָכַלְתָּ֡ לִפְנֵי | יְהֹוָ֣ה אֱלֹהֶ֗יךָ בַּמָּק֣וֹם אֲשֶׁר־יִבְחַר�’ לְשַׁכֵּ֤ן שְׁמוֹ שָׁם מַעְשַׂ֤ר דְּגָֽנְךָ֙ תִּֽירֹשְׁךָ֣ וְיִצְהָרֶ֔ךָ וּבְכֹרֹ֥ת בְּקָֽרְךָ֖ וְצֹאנֶ֑ךָ לְמַ֣עַן תִּלְמַ֗ד לְיִרְאָ֛ה אֶת־יְהֹוָ֥ה אֱלֹהֶ֖יךָ כָּל־הַיָּמִֽים: כד וְכִֽי־יִרְבֶּ֨ה מִמְּךָ֜ הַדֶּ֗רֶךְ כִּ֣י לֹ֤א תוּכַל’ שְׂאֵת֔וֹ כִּֽי־יִרְחַ֤ק מִמְּךָ֙ הַמָּק֔וֹם אֲשֶׁ֤ר יִבְחַר’ יְהֹוָ֣ה אֱלֹהֶ֔יךָ לָשׂ֥וּם שְׁמ֖וֹ שָׁ֑ם כִּ֥י יְבָֽרֶכְךָ֖ יְהֹוָ֥ה אֱלֹהֶֽיךָ: כה וְנָתַתָּ֖ה בַּכָּ֑סֶף וְצַרְתָּ֤ הַכֶּ֙סֶף’ בְּיָ֣דְךָ֔ וְהָֽלַכְתָּ֙ אֶל־הַמָּק֔וֹם אֲשֶׁ֥ר יִבְחַ֛ר יְהֹוָ֥ה אֱלֹהֶ֖יךָ בּֽוֹ: כו וְנָתַתָּ֣ה הַכֶּ֡סֶף בְּכֹל֩ אֲשֶׁר־תְּאַוֶּ֨ה נַפְשְׁךָ֜ בַּבָּקָ֣ר וּבַצֹּ֗אן וּבַיַּ֙יִן’ וּבַשֵּׁכָ֔ר וּבְכֹ֛ל אֲשֶׁ֥ר תִּֽשְׁאָֽלְךָ֖ נַפְשֶׁ֑ךָ וְאָכַ֣לְתָּ שָּׁ֗ם לִפְנֵי’ יְהֹוָ֣ה אֱלֹהֶ֔יךָ וְשָֽׂמַחְתָּ֖ אַתָּ֥ה וּבֵיתֶֽךָ: כז וְהַלֵּוִ֥י אֲשֶׁר־בִּשְׁעָרֶ֖יךָ לֹ֣א תַֽעַזְבֶ֑נּוּ כִּ֣י אֵ֥ין ל֛וֹ חֵ֥לֶק וְנַֽחֲלָ֖ה עִמָּֽךְ: כח מִקְצֵ֣ה | שָׁלֹ֣שׁ שָׁנִ֗ים תּוֹצִיא’ אֶת־כָּל־מַעְשַׂר’ תְּבוּ֣אָֽתְךָ֔ בַּשָּׁנָ֖ה הַהִ֑וא וְהִנַּחְתָּ֖ בִּשְׁעָרֶֽיךָ: כט וּבָ֣א הַלֵּוִ֡י כִּ֣י אֵֽין־לוֹ֩ חֵ֨לֶק וְנַֽחֲלָ֜ה עִמָּ֗ךְ וְ֠הַגֵּ֠ר וְהַיָּת֤וֹם וְהָֽאַלְמָנָה’ אֲשֶׁ֣ר בִּשְׁעָרֶ֔יךָ וְאָֽכְל֖וּ וְשָׂבֵ֑עוּ לְמַ֤עַן יְבָֽרֶכְךָ֙ יְהֹוָ֣ה אֱלֹהֶ֔יךָ בְּכָל־מַֽעֲשֵׂ֥ה יָֽדְךָ֖ אֲשֶׁ֥ר תַּֽעֲשֶֽׂה:

לְמַ֣עַן תִּלְמַ֗ד לְיִרְאָ֛ה אֶת־יְהֹוָ֥ה אֱלֹהֶ֖יךָ כָּל־הַיָּמִֽים

so that you may learn to revere the Lord your God forever

If there is to be a new world, God must be freed from His prison;
He must be led out of the synagogues, out of the churches, out of the
Prayer Book. He must be allowed to live with us. We must make Him
feel at home in our houses, in our shops and offices, in our factories and

Day 2 Torah Reading
Read outside of Israel

On Shabbat start with Deuteronomy Chapter 14:22–29 until Chapter 15:1–18

On a weekday start with Deuteronomy Chapter 15:19–16:17; Maftir: Numbers 28:26–31; Haftarah: Habakkuk 2:20–3:19 (page 125)

First Aliyah When Second Day Falls on Shabbat
Deuteronomy Chapter 14

²² You shall set aside every year a tenth part of all the yield of your sowing that is brought from the field. ²³ You shall consume the tithes of your new grain and wine and oil, and the firstlings of your herds and flocks, in the presence of the Lord your God, in the place where He will choose to establish His name, **so that you may learn to revere the Lord your God forever.** ²⁴ Should the distance be too great for you, should you be unable to transport them, because the place where the Lord your God has chosen to establish His name is far from you and because the Lord your God has blessed you, i.e., with abundant crops – ²⁵ you may convert them into money. Wrap up the money and take it with you to the place that the Lord your God has chosen, ²⁶ and spend the money on anything you want – cattle, sheep, wine, or other intoxicant, or anything you may desire. And you shall feast there, in the presence of the Lord your God, and rejoice with your household. ²⁷ But do not neglect the Levite in your community, for he has no hereditary portion as you have. ²⁸ Every third year you shall bring out the full tithe of your yield of that year, but leave it within your settlements. ²⁹ Then the Levite, who has no hereditary portion as you have, and the stranger, the fatherless, and the widow in your settlements shall come and eat their fill, so that the Lord your God may bless you in all the enterprises you undertake.

---

workshops; everywhere, in every little corner of human life, there must be a place for Him. The preamble to all the blueprints of a better world is: "the beginning of all wisdom is the fear of God" (Psalms 111:10).

Between Yesterday and Tomorrow, page 105

שני כשחל בשבת
דברים פרק טו

מִקֵּץ שֶׁבַע־שָׁנִים תַּעֲשֶׂה שְׁמִטָּה: בּוְזֶה דְּבַר הַשְּׁמִטָּה שָׁמוֹט כָּל־בַּעַל מַשֵּׁה יָדוֹ אֲשֶׁר יַשֶּׁה בְּרֵעֵהוּ לֹא־יִגֹּשׂ אֶת־רֵעֵהוּ וְאֶת־אָחִיו כִּי־קָרָא שְׁמִטָּה לַיהוָה: גאֶת־הַנָּכְרִי תִּגֹּשׂ וַאֲשֶׁר יִהְיֶה לְךָ אֶת־אָחִיךָ תַּשְׁמֵט יָדֶךָ: דאֶפֶס כִּי לֹא יִהְיֶה־בְּךָ אֶבְיוֹן כִּי־בָרֵךְ יְבָרֶכְךָ יהוָה בָּאָרֶץ אֲשֶׁר יהוָה אֱלֹהֶיךָ נֹתֵן־לְךָ נַחֲלָה לְרִשְׁתָּהּ: הרַק אִם־שָׁמוֹעַ תִּשְׁמַע בְּקוֹל יהוָה אֱלֹהֶיךָ לִשְׁמֹר לַעֲשׂוֹת אֶת־כָּל־הַמִּצְוָה הַזֹּאת אֲשֶׁר אָנֹכִי מְצַוְּךָ הַיּוֹם: וכִּי־יהוָה אֱלֹהֶיךָ בֵּרַכְךָ כַּאֲשֶׁר דִּבֶּר־לָךְ וְהַעֲבַטְתָּ גּוֹיִם רַבִּים וְאַתָּה לֹא תַעֲבֹט וּמָשַׁלְתָּ בְּגוֹיִם רַבִּים וּבְךָ לֹא יִמְשֹׁלוּ: {ס} זכִּי־יִהְיֶה בְךָ אֶבְיוֹן מֵאַחַד אַחֶיךָ בְּאַחַד שְׁעָרֶיךָ בְּאַרְצְךָ אֲשֶׁר־יהוָה אֱלֹהֶיךָ נֹתֵן לָךְ לֹא תְאַמֵּץ אֶת־לְבָבְךָ וְלֹא תִקְפֹּץ אֶת־יָדְךָ מֵאָחִיךָ הָאֶבְיוֹן: חכִּי־פָתֹחַ תִּפְתַּח אֶת־יָדְךָ לוֹ וְהַעֲבֵט תַּעֲבִיטֶנּוּ דֵּי מַחְסֹרוֹ אֲשֶׁר יֶחְסַר לוֹ: טהִשָּׁמֶר לְךָ פֶּן־יִהְיֶה דָבָר עִם־לְבָבְךָ בְלִיַּעַל לֵאמֹר קָרְבָה שְׁנַת־הַשֶּׁבַע שְׁנַת הַשְּׁמִטָּה וְרָעָה עֵינְךָ

כָּל־בַּעַל מַשֵּׁה יָדוֹ אֲשֶׁר יַשֶּׁה בְּרֵעֵהוּ לֹא־יִגֹּשׂ אֶת־רֵעֵהוּ וְאֶת־אָחִיו כִּי־קָרָא שְׁמִטָּה לַיהוָה
every creditor shall remit the due that he claims from his fellow; he shall not press his fellow or kinsman, for the remission proclaimed is of the Lord

A very famous case of a halachic problem and its solution is Hillel's *prosbul*. To put it concisely and perhaps not quite accurately, it was the transformation of private debts into public debts. Otherwise, in accordance with the written law of the Bible, these debts would have been forfeited in the *shemittah* year. This was a bold innovation, which Samuel, of a later generation, would have liked to abolish. How and why was it instituted by the great Hillel? He was committed to the law of the *shemittah*. But in his time, this law came into conflict with other valid concerns of Judaism. On the one hand, there was a Torah obligation to protect the interests of the poor who, as the seventh year was approaching, could not obtain any loans for fear that in the *shemittah* year the money would be lost. On the other hand, there was also

SECOND ALIYAH WHEN SECOND DAY FALLS ON SHABBAT
DEUTERONOMY CHAPTER 15

Every seventh year – you shall practice remission of debts. [2] This shall be the nature of the remission: **every creditor shall remit the due that he claims from his fellow; he shall not press his fellow or kinsman, for the remission proclaimed is of the Lord.** [3] You may dun the foreigner; but you must remit whatever is due you from your kinsmen. [4] There shall be no needy among you – since the Lord your God will bless you in the land that the Lord your God is giving you as a hereditary portion – [5] if only you heed the Lord your God and take care to keep all this Instruction that I enjoin upon you this day. [6] For the Lord your God will bless you as He has promised you: you will extend loans to many nations, but require none yourself; you will dominate many nations, but they will not dominate you. [7] If, there is a destitute person among you, one of your brothers in any of your settlements in the land that the Lord your God is giving you, do not harden your heart and shut your hand against your needy kinsman. [8] Rather, you shall surely open your hand to him and lend him sufficient for whatever he needs. [9] Beware lest you harbor the base thought, "The seventh year, the year of remission, is approaching," so that you are mean to

---

the important practical consideration for the effective functioning of the economic process within society, which is also a valid concern of Judaism. Rav Hisda expressed the meaning of the term *prosbul* with an etymologically monstrous, yet essentially correct interpretation: *pros bulee ubutee*, an ordinance in the interest of the poor and the rich (Gittin 36b, 37a). Where did Hillel find the authority for his innovation? Where was it written in the Torah? It was, of course, not found in any text, in any code. He found it within himself. There was a clash between equally valid laws, principles, and concerns of the Torah. He had to find a resolution to the conflict. There was no text, no *Torah shebiktav* to tell him which course to follow. He could find the solution to the problem within his own understanding of the comprehensive ethos of Judaism as he was able to gather it in his own heart and in his own conscience from the totality of the Torah-teaching and the Torah-way of life.

Crisis and Faith, pages 86–87

בְּאָחִ֙יךָ֙ הָֽאֶבְי֔וֹן וְלֹ֣א תִתֵּ֣ן ל֑וֹ וְקָרָ֤א עָלֶ֙יךָ֙ אֶל־יְהֹוָ֔ה וְהָיָ֥ה בְךָ֖ חֵֽטְא׃ נָת֤וֹן
תִּתֵּן֙ ל֔וֹ וְלֹא־יֵרַ֥ע לְבָבְךָ֖ בְּתִתְּךָ֣ ל֑וֹ כִּ֞י בִּגְלַ֣ל ׀ הַדָּבָ֣ר הַזֶּ֗ה יְבָרֶכְךָ֙ יְהֹוָ֣ה
אֱלֹהֶ֔יךָ בְּכׇֽל־מַעֲשֶׂ֔ךָ וּבְכֹ֖ל מִשְׁלַ֥ח יָדֶֽךָ׃ כִּ֛י לֹא־יֶחְדַּ֥ל אֶבְי֖וֹן מִקֶּ֣רֶב
הָאָ֑רֶץ עַל־כֵּ֞ן אָנֹכִ֤י מְצַוְּךָ֙ לֵאמֹ֔ר פָּ֠תֹ֠חַ תִּפְתַּ֨ח אֶת־יָֽדְךָ֜ לְאָחִ֧יךָ לַעֲנִיֶּ֛ךָ
וּלְאֶבְיֹנְךָ֖ בְּאַרְצֶֽךָ׃ {ס} כִּֽי־יִמָּכֵ֨ר לְךָ֜ אָחִ֣יךָ הָֽעִבְרִ֗י א֚וֹ הָֽעִבְרִיָּ֔ה וַעֲבָֽדְךָ֖
שֵׁ֣שׁ שָׁנִ֑ים וּבַשָּׁנָה֙ הַשְּׁבִיעִ֔ת תְּשַׁלְּחֶ֥נּוּ חׇפְשִׁ֖י מֵעִמָּֽךְ׃ וְכִֽי־תְשַׁלְּחֶ֥נּוּ חׇפְשִׁ֖י
מֵעִמָּ֑ךְ לֹ֥א תְשַׁלְּחֶ֖נּוּ רֵיקָֽם׃ הַעֲנֵ֤יק תַּעֲנִיק֙ ל֔וֹ מִצֹּֽאנְךָ֖ וּמִֽגׇּרְנְךָ֣ וּמִיִּקְבֶ֑ךָ
אֲשֶׁ֧ר בֵּרַכְךָ֛ יְהֹוָ֥ה אֱלֹהֶ֖יךָ תִּתֶּן־לֽוֹ׃ וְזָ֣כַרְתָּ֗ כִּ֣י עֶ֙בֶד֙ הָיִ֙יתָ֙ בְּאֶ֣רֶץ מִצְרַ֔יִם
וַֽיִּפְדְּךָ֖ יְהֹוָ֣ה אֱלֹהֶ֑יךָ עַל־כֵּ֞ן אָנֹכִ֧י מְצַוְּךָ֛ אֶת־הַדָּבָ֥ר הַזֶּ֖ה הַיּֽוֹם׃ וְהָיָה֙
כִּֽי־יֹאמַ֣ר אֵלֶ֔יךָ לֹ֥א אֵצֵ֖א מֵעִמָּ֑ךְ כִּ֤י אֲהֵֽבְךָ֙ וְאֶת־בֵּיתֶ֔ךָ כִּי־ט֥וֹב ל֖וֹ עִמָּֽךְ׃
וְלָקַחְתָּ֣ אֶת־הַמַּרְצֵ֗עַ וְנָתַתָּ֤ה בְאׇזְנוֹ֙ וּבַדֶּ֔לֶת וְהָיָ֥ה לְךָ֖ עֶ֣בֶד עוֹלָ֑ם וְאַ֥ף
לַאֲמָתְךָ֖ תַּעֲשֶׂה־כֵּֽן׃ לֹא־יִקְשֶׁ֣ה בְעֵינֶ֗ךָ בְּשַׁלֵּחֲךָ֙ אֹת֤וֹ חׇפְשִׁי֙ מֵֽעִמָּ֔ךְ כִּ֗י
מִשְׁנֶה֙ שְׂכַ֣ר שָׂכִ֔יר עֲבָֽדְךָ֖ שֵׁ֣שׁ שָׁנִ֑ים וּבֵֽרַכְךָ֙ יְהֹוָ֣ה אֱלֹהֶ֔יךָ בְּכֹ֖ל אֲשֶׁ֥ר
תַּעֲשֶֽׂה׃ {פ}

ראשון (שלישי כשחל בשבת)

כׇּֽל־הַבְּכ֡וֹר אֲשֶׁר֩ יִוָּלֵ֨ד בִּבְקׇרְךָ֤ וּבְצֹֽאנְךָ֙ הַזָּכָ֔ר תַּקְדִּ֕ישׁ לַיהֹוָ֖ה אֱלֹהֶ֑יךָ

---

he shall serve you six years　　　　　וַעֲבָֽדְךָ֖ שֵׁ֣שׁ שָׁנִ֑ים

That a Jew should buy another Jew as a slave is an intolerable thought which is rejected by everything that the teaching of the Torah in its religious and ethical significance stands for, yet it was a fact accepted and incorporated in a law. (Exodus 21:1–6). Obviously, slavery was an institution that in biblical times, given human nature, social and economic conditions, could not have been abolished by any law. So the law limited the duration of the slavery. The slave had to be set free after six years of service. The Bible insists on calling the slave "thy brother," and prescribes how he is to be treated: "Thou shalt not rule over him with rigor; but shalt fear thy God" (Leviticus 25:39–43). The rabbis in the Talmud then went on to explain that the slave's standard of living had

your needy kinsman and give him nothing. He will cry out to the Lord against you, and you will incur guilt. [10] Give to him readily and have no regrets when you do so, for in return the Lord your God will bless you in all your efforts and in all your undertakings. [11] For there will never cease to be needy ones in your land, which is why I command you: open your hand to the poor and needy kinsman in your land. [12] If a fellow Hebrew, man or woman, is sold to you, **he shall serve you six years**, and in the seventh year you shall set him free. [13] When you set him free, do not let him go empty-handed: [14] Furnish him out of the flock, threshing floor, and vat, with which the Lord your God has blessed you. [15] Bear in mind that you were slaves in the land of Egypt and the Lord your God redeemed you; therefore I enjoin this commandment upon you today. [16] But should he say to you, "I do not want to leave you" – for he loves you and your household and is happy with you – [17] you shall take an awl and put it through his ear into the door, and he shall become your slave in perpetuity. Do the same with your female slave. [18] When you do set him free, do not feel aggrieved; for in the six years he has given you double the service of a hired man. Moreover, the Lord your God will bless you in all you do.

First Aliyah (on Shabbat, Third Aliyah)

[19] Every firstborn male that is born of your cattle or of your flock **you shall sanctify to the Lord, your God.** You shall neither work with

---

to be equal to that of the master. "Do not yourself eat fine bread and give him the coarse one. Do not you drink old wine and let him have only new wine. Sleep not on a soft bed, while he has to sleep on straw. So much so that people would say: 'He who buys himself a Jewish slave buys a master for himself.'" (Kiddushin 22a).

Crisis and Faith, pages 111–112

you shall sanctify to the Lord, your God　　　　תַּקְדִּישׁ לַיהוָה אֱלֹהֶיךָ

While the concept of choosing does imply "singling out" and "separating from," it is not yet sanctification. Sanctification consists of bringing near, establishing the relation, the closeness of association. To single out

לֹא תַעֲבֹד֙ בִּבְכֹ֣ר שׁוֹרֶ֔ךָ וְלֹ֥א תָגֹ֖ז בְּכ֣וֹר צֹאנֶֽךָ: כלִפְנֵ֩י יְהֹוָ֨ה אֱלֹהֶ֤יךָ תֹאכְלֶ֨נּוּ֙ שָׁנָ֣ה בְשָׁנָ֔ה בַּמָּק֖וֹם אֲשֶׁר־יִבְחַ֣ר יְהֹוָ֑ה אַתָּ֖ה וּבֵיתֶֽךָ: כאוְכִֽי־יִהְיֶ֨ה ב֜וֹ מ֗וּם פִּסֵּ֨חַ֙ א֣וֹ עִוֵּ֔ר כֹּ֖ל מ֣וּם רָ֑ע לֹ֣א תִזְבָּחֶ֔נּוּ לַיהֹוָ֖ה אֱלֹהֶֽיךָ: כבבִּשְׁעָרֶ֖יךָ תֹּֽאכְלֶ֑נּוּ הַטָּמֵ֤א וְהַטָּהוֹר֙ יַחְדָּ֔ו כַּצְּבִ֖י וְכָֽאַיָּֽל: כגרַ֥ק אֶת־דָּמ֖וֹ לֹ֣א תֹאכֵ֑ל עַל־הָאָ֥רֶץ תִּשְׁפְּכֶ֖נּוּ כַּמָּֽיִם:

שני (רביעי כשחל בשבת)
דברים פרק טז

שָׁמוֹר֙ אֶת־חֹ֣דֶשׁ הָֽאָבִ֔יב וְעָשִׂ֣יתָ פֶּ֔סַח לַיהֹוָ֖ה אֱלֹהֶ֑יךָ כִּ֞י בְּחֹ֣דֶשׁ הָֽאָבִ֗יב הוֹצִ֨יאֲךָ֜ יְהֹוָ֧ה אֱלֹהֶ֛יךָ מִמִּצְרַ֖יִם לָֽיְלָה: בוְזָֽבַחְתָּ֥ פֶּ֛סַח לַיהֹוָ֥ה אֱלֹהֶ֖יךָ צֹ֣אן וּבָקָ֑ר בַּמָּקוֹם֙ אֲשֶׁר־יִבְחַ֣ר יְהֹוָ֔ה לְשַׁכֵּ֥ן שְׁמ֖וֹ שָֽׁם: גלֹֽא־תֹאכַ֤ל עָלָיו֙ חָמֵ֔ץ שִׁבְעַ֥ת יָמִ֛ים תֹּֽאכַל־עָלָ֥יו מַצּ֖וֹת לֶ֣חֶם עֹ֑נִי כִּ֣י בְחִפָּז֗וֹן יָצָ֨אתָ֙ מֵאֶ֣רֶץ מִצְרַ֔יִם לְמַ֣עַן תִּזְכֹּ֗ר אֶת־י֤וֹם צֵֽאתְךָ֙ מֵאֶ֣רֶץ מִצְרַ֔יִם כֹּ֖ל יְמֵ֥י חַיֶּֽיךָ:

---

or separate or to withdraw from is a necessary prerequisite of sanctification. This is, in fact, explicitly so stated in Chronicles 1, where it is said of the appointment of Aaron: "and Aaron was separated that he should be sanctified as most holy." (Chronicles 1, 23:13; also Chronicles 2, 7:16). Separation is quite clearly not sanctification; it is a precondition for sanctification. The holy is separated away, but it is not holy because of its separation. It is holy because it is near, because it is close to God. It can be close because it is withdrawn from association and involvements that would render nearness to God impossible.

Man and God, pages 180–181

and make the Passover offering to the Lord   וְעָשִׂ֣יתָ פֶּ֔סַח לַיהֹוָ֖ה אֱלֹהֶ֑יךָ

It is said: "Rabbi Samuel, the Son of Nahman, said in the name of Rabbi Jonathan ... At the time of the destruction of the Egyptians in the Red Sea, the administering angels were about to chant their appointed hymn before the Holy One, blessed be He. Said to them the Holy One, blessed be He: the works of My hands are drowning in the sea and you dare sing My praise before Me!" (Sanhedrin 39b). The same thought found a somewhat different formulation in a probably much

the firstborn of your ox, nor shear the firstborn of your flock. [20] You shall eat it before the Lord, your God, year by year, in the place the Lord chooses – you and your household. [21] And if there be any blemish in it, whether it be lame, or blind, or any ill blemish, you shall not sacrifice it to the Lord, your God. [22] You shall eat it within your cities, the unclean and the clean together, as the deer, and as the gazelle. [23] However, you shall not eat its blood; you shall pour it on the ground, as water.

SECOND ALIYAH (ON SHABBAT, FOURTH ALIYAH)
DEUTERONOMY CHAPTER 16

Keep the month of spring, **and make the Passover offering to the Lord**, your God, for in the month of spring, the Lord, your God, brought you out of Egypt at night. [2] You shall slaughter the Passover sacrifice to the Lord, your God, [of the] flock, and [the Festival sacrifices of the] cattle, in the place which the Lord will choose to establish His Name therein. [3] You shall not eat leaven with it; for seven days you shall eat with it matzoth, the bread of affliction, for in haste you went out of the land of Egypt, so that you shall remember the day when you went out of the land of Egypt all the days of your life.

---

older, anonymous Midrash. It is asked why the expression of rejoicing does not occur in the Bible in connection with the Passover festival, whereas it does occur several times in the description of the observance of the other two (Shavuot and Sukkot) festivals. And the answer is given: "Because the Egyptians died during Passover.... Similarly, you also find that on the occasion of Passover the Hallel (the traditional festival hymn in praise of God) is said only the first night and the first day, but not the other six days as is customary during the seven days of the Sukkot festival. Why so? Because it is said (Proverbs 24:17): 'Rejoice not when thine enemy falleth, and let not thy heart be glad when he stumbles.'" (See Yalkut Shimoni, on Leviticus 23:40). To this day, only "half Hallel" is recited at the Passover services on the last six days of the festival. (For another reason of this custom, however, see Erchin 10a/b). History is not a Sunday school; there is guilt in it and judgment too. But all judgment is tragedy, even if it be as well-deserved as Jews

שלישי (חמישי כשחל בשבת)

וְלֹא־יֵרָאֶה לְךָ שְׂאֹר בְּכָל־גְּבֻלְךָ שִׁבְעַת יָמִים וְלֹא־יָלִין מִן־הַבָּשָׂר אֲשֶׁר תִּזְבַּח בָּעֶרֶב בַּיּוֹם הָרִאשׁוֹן לַבֹּקֶר: הֵלֹא תוּכַל לִזְבֹּחַ אֶת־הַפָּסַח בְּאַחַד שְׁעָרֶיךָ אֲשֶׁר־יְהֹוָה אֱלֹהֶיךָ נֹתֵן לָךְ: כִּי אִם־אֶל־הַמָּקוֹם אֲשֶׁר־יִבְחַר יְהֹוָה אֱלֹהֶיךָ לְשַׁכֵּן שְׁמוֹ שָׁם תִּזְבַּח אֶת־הַפֶּסַח בָּעָרֶב כְּבוֹא הַשֶּׁמֶשׁ מוֹעֵד צֵאתְךָ מִמִּצְרָיִם: וּבִשַּׁלְתָּ וְאָכַלְתָּ בַּמָּקוֹם אֲשֶׁר יִבְחַר יְהֹוָה אֱלֹהֶיךָ בּוֹ וּפָנִיתָ בַבֹּקֶר וְהָלַכְתָּ לְאֹהָלֶיךָ: שֵׁשֶׁת יָמִים תֹּאכַל מַצּוֹת וּבַיּוֹם הַשְּׁבִיעִי עֲצֶרֶת לַיהֹוָה אֱלֹהֶיךָ לֹא תַעֲשֶׂה מְלָאכָה:

רביעי (ששי כשחל בשבת)

שִׁבְעָה שָׁבֻעֹת תִּסְפָּר־לָךְ מֵהָחֵל חֶרְמֵשׁ בַּקָּמָה תָּחֵל לִסְפֹּר שִׁבְעָה

---

believed the judgment of ancient Egypt to be. Judgment is a cosmic tragedy, for it is always on "the works of His hands" that it is executed.

Judaism; Fossil or Ferment, page 75

You shall count seven weeks for yourself　　שִׁבְעָה שָׁבֻעֹת תִּסְפָּר־לָךְ

"And you shall count unto you from the morrow after the day of rest, from the day that you brought the sheaf of the wave offering; seven sabbaths shall there be complete" (Leviticus 23:15).

We still remember with what deep devotion Jewish mystics used to fulfill this seemingly not very significant commandment of counting days and weeks. One day, another, and yet another day ... One week, a second one, and still one more.... Quite so, one may say, but what is the point? Why this intense concentration, which in bygone days used to be applied to a very simple mathematical exercise? The mathematics are all right. Seven days certainly are a week, and fourteen of them do make a fortnight. But what of it?

This is a very good question indeed, especially if it is understood in its widest sense.

The mathematics are all right, but what of it? This is just the question of our times. It is the ominous question mark behind this so-called civilization of ours, which is going to pieces before our own eyes. Only if

Third Aliyah (on Shabbat, Fifth Aliyah)

[4] And no leaven shall be seen with you within all your border for seven days; neither shall any of the flesh you slaughter on the preceding day in the afternoon, remain all night until the morning. [5] You shall not sacrifice the Passover offering within any of your cities, which the Lord, your God, is giving you. [6] Except at the place which the Lord, your God, will choose to establish His Name – there you shall slaughter the Passover offering in the afternoon, as the sun sets, at the appointed time that you went out of Egypt. [7] And you shall roast [it] and eat [it] in the place which the Lord, your God, will choose, and you shall turn away in the morning and go to your dwellings. [8] For six days you shall eat matzoth, and on the seventh day there shall be a halt to the Lord, your God. You shall not do any work [on it].

Fourth Aliyah (On Shabbat Sixth Aliyah)

[9] **You shall count seven weeks for yourself**; from [the time] the sickle is first put to the standing crop, you shall begin to count seven

---

we understand the whole import of this question are we able to realize the meaning of a mathematical process that counts days and weeks, preparing a world which is to be built on the Revelation on Sinai.

I venture to affirm that what men count and how they use their mathematical talent makes all the difference in the world.

We usually think we have succeeded if we can express our achievements in numbers; in numbers of pounds and shillings, in numbers of "hands" which we keep at work, in the number of the shop windows which we own. We think we are getting on in life if the numbers over which we have control are rising. Most of us are possessed by a consuming passion for counting. Most of us are toiling all day long, to be able to sit down in the evening to count and count and count. We are so busy counting and slaving in the thraldom of the number that only very seldom does it occur to us to ask the question: What is the sense of all this counting? It seldom occurs to us that while we are busy creating sums, and new numbers, days and weeks and years pass, days and weeks and years of our short lives which will never come back again. And when we arrive at the end of our life's journey and look back and draw up the great balance sheet and once more check all the accounts

שָׁבֻעוֹת: יִוְעָשִׂיתָ חַג שָׁבֻעוֹת לַיהוָה אֱלֹהֶיךָ מִסַּת נִדְבַת יָדְךָ אֲשֶׁר תִּתֵּן כַּאֲשֶׁר יְבָרֶכְךָ יְהוָה אֱלֹהֶיךָ: יאוְשָׂמַחְתָּ לִפְנֵי | יְהוָה אֱלֹהֶיךָ אַתָּה וּבִנְךָ וּבִתְּךָ וְעַבְדְּךָ וַאֲמָתֶךָ וְהַלֵּוִי אֲשֶׁר בִּשְׁעָרֶיךָ וְהַגֵּר וְהַיָּתוֹם וְהָאַלְמָנָה אֲשֶׁר בְּקִרְבֶּךָ בַּמָּקוֹם אֲשֶׁר־יִבְחַר יְהוָה אֱלֹהֶיךָ לְשַׁכֵּן שְׁמוֹ שָׁם: יבוְזָכַרְתָּ כִּי־ עֶבֶד הָיִיתָ בְּמִצְרָיִם וְשָׁמַרְתָּ וְעָשִׂיתָ אֶת־הַחֻקִּים הָאֵלֶּה:

and are able to convince ourselves that all our life long we were good mathematicians and succeeded in piling up numbers upon numbers, then – notwithstanding all our successes most of us do not feel very happy. Usually, we feel empty and miserable and lonely, and deep down in our hearts we know that, in spite of all our mathematical ingenuity, there was a miscalculation somewhere in life.

The miscalculation is to be seen in the fact that this mathematical civilization never heeded the biblical commandment of counting. Let us consider it now anew.

I suggest we read and translate it as follows. And you shall count unto you. ... And you shall count days and weeks ... that your days on earth may be complete.

You shall count, yes. There is no other way of organizing life efficiently but by counting. We must not forget our mathematics. But "You shall count unto you," i.e., all your countings should be related to "you," to man; to the true needs of man and not to his ambitions, vanities, and passions. You shall count, yes. But do not forget to count and to measure and to weigh yourself with open and critical eyes. You shall count, certainly. But do not forget to take stock of the greatest fortune a man possesses, do not forget to count the days of your life. Did you work all day to amass new sums? Do not sit down in the evening to count the sums and numbers you made; first go into a quiet corner and say: This was one whole day of my short life. Ponder on the day, how you spent it. Was there any sense in it? And how are you to use the fruits of your

weeks. [10] And you shall perform the **Festival of Weeks** to the Lord, your God, the donation you can afford to give, according to how the Lord, your God, shall bless you. [11] And you shall rejoice before the Lord, your God – you, and your son, and your daughter, and your manservant, and your maidservant, and the Levite who is within your cities, and the stranger, and the orphan, and the widow, who are among you, in the place which the Lord, your God, will choose to establish His Name therein. [12] And you shall remember that you were a slave in Egypt, and you shall keep and perform these statutes.

---

toiling so that your work may not be the wasting of your days but the fulness of a life lived to some reasonable end and a satisfactory purpose?

That is how you should count ... that the days of your life may be complete; not rich, nor mighty or powerful, but complete; that there may be completeness, harmony, and perfection in human life.

Between Yesterday and Tomorrow, pages 39, 43–44

Festival of Weeks   חַג שָׁבְעוֹת

Rulings based on feasibility are not to be separated from moral considerations. The idea found its classical expression in a comment by R. Shimon concerning the festivals. As he explained it, the festivals of Passover and Sukkot last seven and eight days, respectively, but the festival of Shavuot lasts only one day. Why? In the spring, when Passover falls, as well as around Sukkot, after the harvest, there is little work in the fields; therefore, let them celebrate for eight days. But Shavuot falls in the busiest work season of the year. One day of festival will suffice. According to R. Shimon, in a spirit similar to that of the Torah's concern for the property of the people, this too teaches us that the Torah is protective toward Israel (Sifrei, Re'eh 16:13). Concern about the material welfare of society is not materialism, but an expression of moral responsibility for the life of the people.

Not in Heaven, pages 26–27

חמישי (שביעי כשחל בשבת)

יג חַג הַסֻּכֹּת תַּעֲשֶׂה לְךָ שִׁבְעַת יָמִים בְּאָסְפְּךָ מִגׇּרְנְךָ וּמִיִּקְבֶךָ: יד וְשָׂמַחְתָּ בְּחַגֶּךָ אַתָּה וּבִנְךָ וּבִתֶּךָ וְעַבְדְּךָ וַאֲמָתֶךָ וְהַלֵּוִי וְהַגֵּר וְהַיָּתוֹם וְהָאַלְמָנָה אֲשֶׁר בִּשְׁעָרֶיךָ: טו שִׁבְעַת יָמִים תָּחֹג לַיהֹוָה אֱלֹהֶיךָ בַּמָּקוֹם אֲשֶׁר־יִבְחַר יְהֹוָה כִּי יְבָרֶכְךָ יְהֹוָה אֱלֹהֶיךָ בְּכֹל תְּבוּאָתְךָ וּבְכֹל מַעֲשֵׂה יָדֶיךָ וְהָיִיתָ אַךְ שָׂמֵחַ: טז שָׁלוֹשׁ פְּעָמִים | בַּשָּׁנָה יֵרָאֶה כׇל־זְכוּרְךָ אֶת־פְּנֵי | יְהֹוָה אֱלֹהֶיךָ בַּמָּקוֹם אֲשֶׁר יִבְחָר בְּחַג הַמַּצּוֹת וּבְחַג הַשָּׁבֻעוֹת וּבְחַג הַסֻּכּוֹת וְלֹא יֵרָאֶה אֶת־פְּנֵי יְהֹוָה רֵיקָם: יז אִישׁ כְּמַתְּנַת יָדוֹ כְּבִרְכַּת יְהֹוָה אֱלֹהֶיךָ אֲשֶׁר נָתַן־לָךְ:

Festival of Sukkot   חַג הַסֻּכֹּת

Contrary to Kant, Judaism teaches that man's "true service of God" must be human. It should be invisible, as man's soul is invisible; and it should be visible, too, because man is visible. It must be "service of the heart, in spirit and in truth" as well as of the body. It must be service through the *mitzvah*, the deed in which man's spiritual and material nature have unified. It is a much higher service than that of the spirit alone. It is the religion of the whole man.

Bahya ibn Pakuda differentiated between "duties of the heart" and "duties of the body," but only in order to be able to concentrate all the more on the "duties of the heart." In reality, however, the *mitzvah* represents the coalescing of the two categories of duties in the one unifying deed, which should be known as the duty of man.

The essence of such service has been beautifully expressed by a latter-day rabbi, who said that of all those commandments that are "between God and man," he loved most that of dwelling in the sukkah. In entering the sukkah, one steps into the *mitzvah* with one's very boots on. This is, indeed, basic Judaism. It is comparatively easy to relate the spiritual to God; it is as easy as it is ineffective in history. The real task is to orient the whole world of man, matter, and spirit toward God.

God, Man and History, pages 125–126

Fifth Aliyah (On Shabbat Seventh Aliyah)

[13] You shall make yourself the **Festival of Sukkot** for seven days, when you gather in [the produce] from your threshing floor and your vat. [14] **And you shall rejoice in your Festival** – you, and your son, and your daughter, and your manservant, and your maidservant, and the Levite, and the stranger, and the orphan, and the widow, who are within your cities. [15] Seven days you shall celebrate the Festival to the Lord, your God, in the place which the Lord shall choose, because the Lord, your God, will bless you in all your produce, and in all the work of your hands, and you will only be happy. [16] Three times in the year, every one of your males shall appear before the Lord, your God, in the place He will choose: on the Festival of Matzoth and on the Festival of Weeks, and on the Festival of Sukkot, and he shall not appear before the Lord empty-handed. [17] [Every] man [shall bring] as much as he can afford, according to the blessing of the Lord, your God, which He has given you.

And you shall rejoice in your Festival   וְשָׂמַחְתָּ בְּחַגֶּךָ

Sukkot is called "the season of our joy." It used to be a happy time of rejoicing. The hard work of a whole year done, the harvest brought in, the rich blessings of nature well garnered, man could relax. He could thank God with a contented and satisfied mind. But what is the season of our joy today? Where are the great harvests that used to make people happy? There is little "*Simchah*" left in a world in which Death has become the richest harvester. We have forgotten the meaning of joy. It is, however, important to realize that it is not only this war, with its small and great tragedies or the overpowering martyrdom of Israel in its wake, that has caused us to forget the meaning of joy. Long before its outbreak, true joy had left our hearts. Joy, happiness, harmony, contentment, and peace left this world long before the present catastrophe. The generation of those born not many years before 1914 has never really known of these blessings of life. During the two decades between the two wars, the world was in a fever. Many people worked, and others were workless. Many fought for things that they could never achieve; for many, there was success – in a sense. But the place of "*Simchah*"

מפטיר

במדבר פרק כח:כו-לא

כו וּבְי֣וֹם הַבִּכּוּרִ֗ים בְּהַקְרִֽיבְכֶ֞ם מִנְחָ֤ה חֲדָשָׁה֙ לַֽיהֹוָ֔ה בְּשָׁבֻעֹ֖תֵיכֶ֑ם מִקְרָא־קֹ֨דֶשׁ֙ יִהְיֶ֣ה לָכֶ֔ם כָּל־מְלֶ֥אכֶת עֲבֹדָ֖ה לֹ֥א תַעֲשֽׂוּ: כז וְהִקְרַבְתֶּ֨ם עוֹלָ֜ה לְרֵ֣יחַ נִיחֹחַ֮ לַֽיהֹוָה֒ פָּרִ֧ים בְּנֵֽי־בָקָ֛ר שְׁנַ֖יִם אַ֣יִל אֶחָ֑ד שִׁבְעָ֥ה כְבָשִׂ֖ים בְּנֵ֥י שָׁנָֽה: כח וּמִ֨נְחָתָ֔ם סֹ֖לֶת בְּלוּלָ֣ה בַשָּׁ֑מֶן שְׁלֹשָׁ֣ה עֶשְׂרֹנִ֗ים לַפָּר֙ הָֽאֶחָ֔ד שְׁנֵי֙ עֶשְׂרֹנִ֔ים לָאַ֖יִל הָֽאֶחָֽד: כט עִשָּׂרוֹן֙ עִשָּׂר֔וֹן לַכֶּ֖בֶשׂ הָֽאֶחָ֑ד לְשִׁבְעַ֖ת הַכְּבָשִֽׂים: ל שְׂעִ֥יר עִזִּ֛ים אֶחָ֖ד לְכַפֵּ֥ר עֲלֵיכֶֽם: לא מִלְּבַ֞ד עֹלַ֤ת הַתָּמִיד֙ וּמִנְחָת֔וֹ תַּעֲשׂ֑וּ תְּמִימִ֥ם יִֽהְיוּ־לָכֶ֖ם וְנִסְכֵּיהֶֽם:

---

was vacant in the world. Where joy should be in the life of men there was emptiness, disillusionment, and boredom. When people were not working and not busy chasing the mirages of their ambitions, they were not at peace, not happy, but bored. Mere entertainment took the place of joy, entertainment that one buys for money and that is an efficient means of killing time and making a man forget the void within him. A whole entertainment industry had to be produced in a world that, not knowing genuine joy, was bored.

Between Yesterday and Tomorrow, page 136

Maftir Portion
Numbers Chapter 28

[26] And on the day of the first fruits, **when you offer up a new meal offering to the Lord**, on your festival of Weeks; it shall be a holy convocation for you, and you shall not perform any mundane work. [27] You shall offer up a burnt offering with a spirit of satisfaction to the Lord: two young bulls, one ram, and seven lambs in the first year. [28] Their meal offerings [shall be] fine flour mixed with oil; three-tenths for each bull and two-tenths for the ram. [29] One-tenth for each lamb, for all seven lambs. [30] One young male goat to atone for you. [31] You shall offer this up besides the continual burnt offering and its meal offering they shall be unblemished for you, as well as their libations.

וּבְיוֹם הַבִּכּוּרִים בְּהַקְרִיבְכֶם מִנְחָה חֲדָשָׁה לַיהוָה

And on the day of the first fruits, when you offer up a new meal offering to the Lord

In cases where there was no question that the written word might impinge on the human dignity of a person, the halacha was mindful not to allow practices that would shame the ignorant and, especially, the poor. The Bible prescribes the reading of an appropriate text at the annual offering of the first fruits at the Temple in Jerusalem. Originally, those who could read would read the verses themselves. Someone else would read on behalf of those who could not. However, this practice shamed the illiterate, and they refused to come. Thus, a new regulation was introduced: An official of the Temple had to read the prescribed text on behalf of everyone without distinction (Hagiga 3:7).

Not in Heaven, pages 34–35

הפטרה

חבקוק פרק ב

כוַיהוָֹה בְּהֵיכַל קָדְשׁוֹ הַס מִפָּנָיו כָּל־הָאָרֶץ:

חבקוק פרק ג

א‏ּתְפִלָּה לַחֲבַקּוּק הַנָּבִיא עַל שִׁגְיֹנוֹת:

יָצִיב פִּתְגָם. לְאָת וּדְגָם. בְּרִבּוֹ רִבְבָן עִירִין,
עֲנֵי אָנָא. בְּמִנְיָנָא. דְּפָסְלִין אַרְבְּעָה טוּרִין.
קָדָמוֹהִי. לְגוֹ מוֹהִי. נְגִיד וּנְפִיק נְהַר דְּנוּרִין,
בְּטוּר תַּלְגָּא. נְהוֹר שְׁרַגָּא. וְזִיקִין דְּנוּר וּבְעוּרִין.

בְּרָא וּסְכָא. מַה בַּחֲשׁוֹכָא. וְעִמֵּהּ שַׁרְיַן נְהוֹרִין,
רְחִיקִין צָפָא. בְּלָא שִׁטְפָא. וְגַלְיַן לֵהּ דְּמִטַּמְּרִין.
בָּעִית מִנֵּהּ. יָת הָרְמוֹנֶה. וּבְתַרְוֹהִי אֲדֵי גוּבְרִין,
יָדְעֵי הִלְכְתָא. וּמַתְנִיתָא וְתוֹסֶפְתָּא. סִפְרָא וְסִפְרִין.

---

with hidden things revealed to Him   וְגַלְיַן לֵהּ דְּמִטַּמְּרִין

The hiding God is present; though man is unaware of him, He is present in his hiddenness. Therefore, God can only hide in this world. But if this world were altogether and radically profane, there would be no place in it for Him to hide. He can only hide in history. Since history is man's responsibility, one would, in fact, expect him to hide, to be silent, while man is about his God-given task. Responsibility requires freedom, but God's convincing presence would undermine the freedom of

HAFTARAH

HABAKKUK CHAPTER 2

²⁰ But the Lord is in His Holy Temple. Silence the whole earth before Him.

HABAKKUK CHAPTER 3

A prayer of Habakkuk the prophet concerning the errors.

YETZIV PITGAM

Certain is our praise of God, that is but a sign and sample,
of that uttered by myriad myriads of angels,
I shall call out His praise, among the numbered tribes,
that are inscribed in the four rows (of the Kohen Gadol's breastplate).
Before Him, among the water of Paradise, flows and goes a fiery stream,
On a snowy mountain, is a blinding light, and bolts of flaming fire.

He created and sees, what is shrouded in darkness,
because light's essence dwells with Him,
He sees from afar, without hindrance, **with hidden things revealed to Him.**
I seek permission from Him first, and afterwards from people,
Those who know the Law, and Mishnah and Tosefta, Sifra, and Sifrin.

---

human decision. God hides in human responsibility and human freedom. However, where there is no room for history, where redemption lies, not in a process of sanctification, but in the transfiguration of a profane existence into a new birth in eternity, there God cannot hide. He must be visible in the miracle of salvation; he saves by his epiphany.

Faith After the Holocaust, page 63

מֶלֶךְ חַיָּא, לְעָלְמַיָּא, יְמַגֵּן עָם לְהוֹן מְשַׁחֲרִין,
אֲמִיר עֲלֵיהוֹן, כְּחָלָא יְהוֹן, וְלָא יִתְמְנוּן הֵיךְ עַפְרִין,
יְחַוְּרוּן כְּעָן, לְהוֹן בִּקְעָן, יְטוּפוּן נַעֲוֹהִי חַמְרִין,
רְעוּתְהוֹן הַב, וְאַפֵּיהוֹן צְהַב, יְנַהֲרוּן כִּנְהַר צַפְרִין.

לִי הַב תְּקוֹף, וְעֵינָךְ זְקוֹף, חֲזֵי עָרָךְ דְּבָךְ כַּפְרִין,
וִיהוֹן כְּתַבְנָא, בְּגוֹ לִבְנָא, כְּאַבְנָא יִשְׁתָּקוּן חַפְרִין,
יְהוֹנָתָן, גְּבַר עֲנְוְתָן, בְּכֵן לֵהּ נַמְטֵי אַפְרִין.

---

may He shield the people that prays to Him   יְמַגֵּן עָם לְהוֹן מְשַׁחֲרִין

Toward the end of 1938 and early in 1939, there was a case in Berlin of a young woman whose husband was in a mental asylum. Every Jew was trying to get out of Germany. Thus, the woman sought a rabbinical court to arrange a divorce for her, so she could save herself and her five-year-old child. She would not have been leaving her husband in the lurch. She had every moral reason to demand a divorce: Prior to their marriage, he had contracted syphilis. He did not have it treated. By the time of their marriage, the sickness had reached a stage when it was no longer contagious. The man married without informing his bride of the condition of his health. As the years passed, the disease attacked his brain and he became insane. As indicated earlier, an insane person is not competent to authorize the writing and transfer of the divorce document.

The poor woman was running from rabbi to rabbi in Berlin to no avail. No one wanted to touch her case. Finally, someone advised her to seek me out. I was then the youngest rabbi serving the Jewish community, still in my twenties. The first question I asked myself was: Is the halachic concept of incompetence due to insanity identical with the medical definition? I visited the man in the asylum and concluded that, from a halachic point of view, he was quite capable of giving a *get*. Consequently, I wrote a responsum about the case, proving that halachically the husband was competent. I submitted it to Rabbi Yehiel Jacob Weinberg, of blessed memory, the internationally recognized halachic authority. On his visit to Vilna, he discussed the matter with

The King Who lives, eternally, **may He shield the people that pray to Him**,
Say to them, "May they be like the sand, and as uncountable as dust.
May their valleys be covered, with crops as white as sheep,
may their cellars flow with wine."
Grant their wish, and may their faces glow with a brilliance like the light of dawn.

Give me strength, and lift Your eye, to see the enemy who denies You,
Let them be like straw, mixed in with brick, let them be mute as a stone with humiliation.
God presented [the Torah] to (Moses) the epitome of humility,
so let us extend Him gracious praise.

---

the venerable Rabbi Hayim Ozer Grodzinski, of blessed memory, and came back with the message that the latter agreed with my findings. (R. Weinberg published my responsum in his work *Sridei Esh*, vol. 3:35).

[Years later Rabbi Leo Jung of New York approached Rabbi Weinberg, who then lived in Montreux, Switzerland, to propose a solution to the manifold *aguna* problem. In those days Rabbi Weinberg's health had been greatly weakened by his concentration camp experiences. He advised Rabbi Jung to ask me to work on the problem. (I assume the memory of our joint Berlin experience induced him to do so.) In response to this appeal of my revered teacher, I wrote my halachic work *Conditionality in Marriage and Divorce* (Jerusalem: Mosad Harav Kook, 2008) (Hebrew).]

Unfortunately, I was unable to bring the matter to a successful conclusion. First of all, the husband understood the meaning of a *get* so well that he refused to cooperate. Possibly, this difficulty could have been overcome. The technical difficulties were insurmountable – so I felt. One would have had to bring a scribe to the asylum, so the husband could personally authorize him to write the *get*. In addition, two witnesses would have had to be present, and a messenger would have to authorize the husband to hand the *get* to his wife. I felt unable to move the Nazi hospital authorities to help in the matter.

בִּיהֹוָ֖ה שָׁמַ֣עְתִּי שִׁמְעֲךָ֮ יָרֵאתִי֒ יְהֹוָ֗ה פׇּעׇלְךָ֙ בְּקֶ֤רֶב שָׁנִים֙ חַיֵּ֔יהוּ בְּקֶ֧רֶב שָׁנִ֛ים תּוֹדִ֖יעַ בְּרֹ֥גֶז רַחֵ֥ם תִּזְכּֽוֹר: גאֱל֙וֹהַ֙ מִתֵּימָ֣ן יָב֔וֹא וְקָד֥וֹשׁ מֵהַר־פָּארָ֖ן סֶ֑לָה כִּסָּ֤ה שָׁמַ֙יִם֙ הוֹד֔וֹ וּתְהִלָּת֖וֹ מָלְאָ֥ה הָאָֽרֶץ: דוְנֹ֙גַהּ֙ כָּא֣וֹר תִּֽהְיֶ֔ה קַרְנַ֥יִם מִיָּד֖וֹ ל֑וֹ וְשָׁ֖ם חֶבְי֥וֹן עֻזֹּֽה: הלְפָנָ֖יו יֵ֣לֶךְ דָּ֑בֶר וְיֵצֵ֥א רֶ֖שֶׁף לְרַגְלָֽיו: ועָמַ֣ד | וַיְמֹ֣דֶד אֶ֗רֶץ רָאָה֙ וַיַּתֵּ֣ר גּוֹיִ֔ם וַיִּתְפֹּֽצְצוּ֙ הַרְרֵי־עַ֔ד שַׁח֖וּ גִּבְע֣וֹת עוֹלָ֑ם הֲלִיכ֥וֹת עוֹלָ֖ם לֽוֹ: זתַּ֣חַת אָ֔וֶן רָאִ֖יתִי אׇהֳלֵ֣י כוּשָׁ֑ן יִרְגְּז֕וּן יְרִיע֖וֹת אֶ֥רֶץ מִדְיָֽן: חהֲבִנְהָרִים֙ חָרָ֣ה יְהֹוָ֔ה אִ֤ם בַּנְּהָרִים֙ אַפֶּ֔ךָ אִם־בַּיָּ֖ם עֶבְרָתֶ֑ךָ כִּ֤י תִרְכַּב֙ עַל־סוּסֶ֔יךָ מַרְכְּבֹתֶ֖יךָ יְשׁוּעָֽה: טעֶרְיָ֤ה תֵעוֹר֙ קַשְׁתֶּ֔ךָ שְׁבֻע֖וֹת מַטּ֣וֹת אֹ֑מֶר סֶ֖לָה נְהָר֥וֹת תְּבַקַּע־אָֽרֶץ: ירָא֤וּךָ יָחִ֙ילוּ֙ הָרִ֔ים זֶ֥רֶם מַ֖יִם עָבָ֑ר נָתַ֤ן תְּהוֹם֙ קוֹל֔וֹ ר֖וֹם יָדֵ֥יהוּ נָשָֽׂא: יאשֶׁ֥מֶשׁ יָרֵ֖חַ עָ֣מַד זְבֻ֑לָה לְא֤וֹר חִצֶּ֙יךָ֙ יְהַלֵּ֔כוּ לְנֹ֖גַהּ בְּרַ֥ק חֲנִיתֶֽךָ: יבבְּזַ֖עַם תִּצְעַד־אָ֑רֶץ בְּאַ֖ף תָּד֥וּשׁ גּוֹיִֽם: יגיָצָ֙אתָ֙ לְיֵ֣שַׁע עַמֶּ֔ךָ

Eventually, my family and I left Germany, but what became of the poor woman and her child? And yet, all this was unnecessary. It could have been easily prevented. Had I, in those early years of my rabbinical career, had the experience and halachic understanding I acquired later, I would have made the case for annulling her marriage retroactively because the husband had failed to inform her about the state of his health. It would have been relatively easy, under the prevailing conditions, to give the ruling a solid halachic foundation.

Not in Heaven, pages 157–159

In anger You shall remember to have mercy   בְּרֹגֶז רַחֵם תִּזְכּוֹר

According to Jewish tradition, God originally planned to create the world according to his attribute of justice. But he saw that a world ruled by a just God could not exist. He, therefore, let his attribute of mercy precede and, thus, he associated mercy with justice and created the world. What is not stated in the teaching but is implied, is the equally true thought that although it is sure that the world will not stand by divine justice, it is at least extremely doubtful that it could survive by unlimited divine mercy. For it is God's love and mercy that gives men the opportunity for satanic self-assertion and rebellion against God

[2] Lord, I heard a report of You; I feared, Lord, Your deed. In the midst of the years, revive it; in the midst of the years, let it be known. **In anger You shall remember to have mercy.** [3] God came from Teman; yea, the Holy One from Mt. Paran, with everlasting might. His glory covered the heavens and His splendor filled the earth. [4] And there was a brightness like the light; they had rays from His hand, and there was His strength hidden. [5] A pestilence went before Him, and sparks went out at His feet. [6] He stood and meted out to the earth; He saw and caused nations to wander. And the everlasting mountains were shattered; the everlasting hills were humbled. The procedures of the world are His. [7] Because of iniquity I saw the tents of Cushan; the curtains of the land of Midian quaked. [8] Was the Lord angry with the rivers? Is His wrath against the rivers, or His fury against the sea? Only that You rode on Your steeds with Your chariots of salvation. [9] Your bow revealed itself; The oaths to the tribes were a perpetual statement; You split the earth into rivers. [10] Mountains saw You and quaked. A stream of water passed. The deep gave forth its voice. The heaven raised up its thanks. [11] The sun and the moon stood in their dwellings; to the light of Your arrows they go, to the brightness of the lightning of Your spear. [12] With fury You tread the earth; with wrath You trample nations. [13] You went forth to rescue Your people,

---

Himself. Because of God's long-suffering, man may indulge in hubris and get away with it. But hubris too, if it remains unchecked, will destroy man. A world ruled by divine justice would perish because of God's justice; a world ruled by divine mercy would perish because of human hubris. A world of justice could not endure the divine wrath; a world of pure divine long-suffering could not endure man's wrath. There is judgment, but mercy precedes it. Judgment is delayed by divine mercy and forbearance. Because mercy delays judgment, man may indulge in rebellion and become guilty of hubris. Because God is forbearing, man may get away with it for a while. But judgment is only delayed. The man of hubris does not escape nemesis. There is judgment and there is a Judge in world history. The manner of Israel's survival testifies to the long-suffering Judge of history.

Faith after the Holocaust, pages 122–123

לְיֶ֫שַׁע אֶת־מְשִׁיחֶ֑ךָ מָחַ֥צְתָּ רֹּאשׁ֘ מִבֵּ֪ית רָשָׁ֫ע עָר֥וֹת יְס֑וֹד עַד־צַוָּ֣אר סֶֽלָה׃ יֹ‍ד נָקַ֣בְתָּ בְמַטָּיו֮ רֹ֪אשׁ פְּרָ֫זָ֥ו יִסְעֲר֥וּ לַהֲפִיצֵ֑נִי עֲלִ֣יצֹתָ֔ם כְּמוֹ־לֶאֱכֹ֖ל עָנִ֣י בַּמִּסְתָּֽר׃ יֹ‍ה דָּרַ֣כְתָּ בַיָּ֣ם סוּסֶ֑יךָ חֹ֝֗מֶר מַ֣יִם רַבִּֽים׃ יֹ‍ו שָׁמַ֤עְתִּי ׀ וַתִּרְגַּ֬ז בִּטְנִ֗י לְקוֹל֘ צָלֲל֪וּ שְׂפָתַ֫י יָב֥וֹא רָקָ֣ב בַּעֲצָמַ֔י וְתַחְתַּ֖י אֶרְגָּ֑ז אֲשֶׁ֤ר אָנ֙וּחַ֙ לְי֣וֹם צָרָ֔ה לַעֲל֖וֹת לְעַ֥ם יְגוּדֶֽנּוּ׃ יֹ‍ז כִּֽי־תְאֵנָ֣ה לֹֽא־תִפְרָ֗ח וְאֵ֤ין יְבוּל֙ בַּגְּפָנִ֔ים כִּחֵ֖שׁ מַעֲשֵׂה־זַ֔יִת וּשְׁדֵמ֖וֹת לֹא־עָ֣שָׂה אֹ֑כֶל גָּזַ֤ר מִמִּכְלָה֙ צֹ֔אן וְאֵ֥ין בָּקָ֖ר בָּרְפָתִֽים׃ יֹ‍ח וַאֲנִ֖י בַּיהֹוָ֣ה אֶעְל֑וֹזָה אָגִ֖ילָה בֵּאלֹהֵ֥י יִשְׁעִֽי׃ יֹ‍ט יְהֹוִ֤ה אֲדֹנָי֙ חֵילִ֔י וַיָּ֤שֶׂם רַגְלַי֙ כָּֽאַיָּל֔וֹת וְעַ֥ל בָּמוֹתַ֖י יַדְרִכֵ֑נִי לַמְנַצֵּ֖חַ בִּנְגִינוֹתָֽי׃

to rescue Your anointed. You have crushed the head of the house of the wicked, uncovering it from the foundation to the neck – forever. [14] You pierced the heads of his villages with his war clubs. They storm to scatter me. Their joy was when they could devour a poor one in secret. [15] You trampled in the sea with Your steeds, a heap of many waters. [16] I heard, and my inward parts trembled; my lips quivered at the sound. Decay entered my bones, and I quaked in my place, that [the time] I would rest is destined for a day of trouble – to bring up a people that will troop back. [17] For a fig tree shall not blossom; neither is there produce on the vines. The labor of the olive tree shall fail, and the grain field shall not produce food. The flock shall be cut off from the fold, and there shall be no cattle in the stalls. [18] Yet, I will rejoice in the Lord; I will jubilate in the God of my salvation. [19] God the Lord is my strength. He made my feet [as swift] as the deer's, and He guides me on my high places. To the conductor [to play] with my melodies!

Bibliography

BOOKS BY RABBI ELIEZER BERKOVITS QUOTED IN THIS VOLUME

Towards Historic Judaism (Oxford: East and West Library, 1943).

Between Yesterday and Tomorrow. Sermons by Rabbi E. Berkovits (Oxford: East and West Library, 1945).

Judaism: Fossil or Ferment? (New York: Philosophical Library, 1956).

Prayer (New York: Yeshiva University, 1962).

Man and God: Studies in Biblical Theology (Detroit: Wayne State University Press, 1969).

Major Themes in Modern Philosophies of Judaism (New York: Ktav Publishing House, 1974).

Crisis and Faith (New York: Sanhedrin Press, 1976).

With God in Hell: Judaism in the Ghettos and Death Camps (New York: Sanhedrin Press, 1979).

God, Man and History: A Jewish Interpretation (Jerusalem: Shalem Press, 2004) [republished from New York: Jonathan David Publishing, 1959].

Not in Heaven: The Nature and Function of Halakha (Jerusalem: Shalem Press, 2010) [republished from New York: Ktav Publishing House, 1983].

What is the Talmud (Sefaria.org, translation into English, 2013) [republished from Berlin: Erwin Löwe Jewish Book Publishers, 1935].

Faith After the Holocaust (Jerusalem: Maggid Books, 2019) [republished from New York: Ktav Publishing House, 1973].

Jewish Women in Time and Torah (Jerusalem: Urim Publications and Ktav Publishing House, 2022, second edition) [republished from New Jersey: Ktav Publishing House, 1990].

ARTICLE BY RABBI ELIEZER BERKOVITS QUOTED IN THIS VOLUME

"Conversion 'According to Halachah' – What Is It?" *Judaism* (Volume 23 Number 4, Fall 1974) pages 467-478.